FORTY NIGHTS

Creation Centered
Night Prayer

DANIEL J. MCGILL

PAULIST PRESS
New York and Mahwah, N.J.

Book design by Nighthawk Design.

Copyright © 1993 by Daniel J. McGill

Library of Congress Cataloging-in-Publication Data

McGill, Daniel J., 1955–
    Forty nights: creation centered night prayer/
    Daniel J. McGill.
      p. cm.
    ISBN 0-8091-3437-3 (pbk.)
    1. Creation—Prayer-books and devotions—English.
  2. Nature—Prayer-books and devotions—English.
  I. Title. II. Title: Night prayer.
BV4832.2.M1954 1993
242'.8—dc20   93-21386
                                     CIP

Published by Paulist Press
997 Macarthur Boulevard
Mahwah, New Jersey 07430

Printed and bound in the
United States of America

TABLE OF CONTENTS

CONTENTS

CONTENTS

For Charlene McGill,
my mother, who knows prayer's necessity
and the wonder of an open heart and mind

and Ken McGill,
my father, who loves exploring the Earth
as much as attending Sunday mass.

ACKNOWLEDGMENTS

Unless otherwise noted, scripture quotations are from the New Revised Standard Version of the Bible, copyright ©1989 by the Division of Christian Education of the National Council of the Churches of Christ in the USA. Used by Permission. All rights reserved. "The Canticle of the Sun" by Francis of Assisi is taken from *Francis and Clare: The Complete Works* translated by Regis J. Armstrong and Ignatius C. Brady, ©1982 by the Missionary Society of St. Paul the Apostle in the State of New York, reprinted by permission of Paulist Press. The quotation by Aldo Leopold is taken from *A Sand County Almanac,* Oxford University Press. The quotation by Thomas Merton is from *Raids on the Unspeakable* published by New Directions. The quotation by Joseph Wood Krutch is from *The Voice of the Desert,* William Sloan Associates. Material by Thomas Berry is reprinted with permission from *Befriending the Earth: A Theology of Reconciliation between Humans and the Earth* by Thomas Berry, C.P., in dialogue with Thomas E. Clarke, S.J., ©1991 by Holy Cross Center of Ecology and Spirituality, published by Twenty-Third Publications, PO Box 180, Mystic, CT 06355. The Grail translation of Psalm 65 is copyright 1963 by the Ladies of the Grail (England) and reprinted by permission of G.I.A. Publications, Inc., Chicago, IL, exclusive agents. All rights reserved. The quotation from *The Upanishads* by Swami Prabhavananda is taken from the edition published by Vedanta Press, Hollywood, CA. The excerpt "I like to walk alone on country paths. . ." by Thich Nhat Hanh is taken from *The Miracle of Mindfulness* by Thich Nhat Hanh published by Beacon Press, revised edition 1987. Other quotations by the same author are reprinted from *Being Peace* by Thich Nhat Hanh, by permission of Parallax Press, Berkeley, CA, 1987. Selections by Black Elk are reprinted from *Black Elk Speaks* by John G. Neihardt by permission of the University of Nebraska Press, copyright 1932, 1959, 1972 by John G. Neihardt, copyright ©1961 by the John G. Neihardt Trust. Penguin Books Ltd has given permission to reprint selections from *The Narrow Road to the Deep North and Other Travel Sketches* by Basho, translated by Nobuyuki Yuasa (Penguin Classics, 1966), copyright ©1966 by Nobuyuki Yuasa; from *The Bhagavad Gita,* translated

INTRODUCTION

Every scribe who has been trained for the kingdom of heaven is like the master of a household who brings out of his treasure what is new and what is old.

—Matthew 13:52

This book of prayer is a response, a personal response, to the spiritual and intellectual transformation of this age. Even though many may still be unaware of it, or even unconsciously fighting against it, we live at the moment of the most dramatic developments in the history of the planet Earth and of the understanding of the human species upon it. Everywhere humans live, the realization that there is but one Earth, one Universe and one Reality is swallowing the parochial black holes that our minds have lived in since their conception. Environmental awareness, science and ecumenism are literally transforming the human spirit and understanding, and with the human, the planet is transformed as well.

As a Roman Catholic, my primary form of

prayer for years was Night Prayer from the Liturgy of the Hours, a written form of prayer developed primarily for monasteries. Still, much as I love this beautiful prayer, I found that I wanted to include and encounter so much more than Night Prayer offered. And so, timidly, I began to create prayer services for myself, services that included ideas from other religions, great scientists, even agnostics. One by one I created these prayers, finding more and more life in them as I expanded the number of voices speaking in them.

Always I have loved the book of Psalms, which became one of my greatest joys when I wrote my own psalms. Living in the Colorado Plateau desert I wanted to give voice to the wonder of creation here in this land. And from this springboard of a desert land I found myself wanting to celebrate the awesome and wonderful new awareness of life and the universe that is burgeoning in this age.

Yet, like the scribe in the scripture verse above, I love the old treasures of my faith tradition as well, and often found in them uncanny echoes of the new treasures this age is generating.

And so the prayers came, and slowly I began to create my own office of night prayers, but I wondered where it was headed. Then one day an answer came to me in a title, "Forty Nights of Prayer." At the time, I remember it as just sounding catchy. But later I came to realize the significance of the number, the Hebrew number of transformation. Then I realized the journey I was on, a journey of personal transformation.

This book owes an enormous debt to the many saints, poets, authors, translators, editors, and publishers from whose work it has borrowed heavily. I also wish to thank those who gave crucial support to the book directly or indirectly–Barbara and Joe Kerns, Bob and Connie Borchardt, Anne Brost and Mary Glenn at Whitewater Community, Andrew Kemberling of Holy Cross Abbey, Karen and Richard Levad, John Costanzo, my parents, Ken and Charlene McGill, Saint Joseph's Parish in Grand Junction, Colorado, Don Brophy and Kevin Lynch at Paulist Press, my children, Megan and Brendan, who prayed the book with me more than anyone else, and my wife, Lawana, my editor, anchor, and friend.

FORTY NIGHTS

Keep to the Simple

◗ ◖

OPENING

God, listen to my prayer!
—**Send forth your Spirit and renew the face of the Earth.**

PSALM

Psalm 134

Antiphon: **In the silent hours of night, bless the LORD.**

Come, bless the LORD, all you servants of the
    LORD,
who stand by night in the house of the LORD!

Lift up your hands to the holy place,
    and bless the LORD.

May the LORD, maker of heaven and Earth,
   bless you from Zion.

Antiphon: **In the silent hours of night, bless the LORD.**

READING

The highest good is like water.
Water gives life to everything
   and does not compete with any
It flows in the places people reject
And so it is like the Tao.

In dwelling, care about the land.
In thought, go deep.
In relationships, be generous and kind.
In words, speak truth.
In government, seek harmony and accord.
In what you do, be skilled.
In action, be aware and present.

When you do not compete, you are without fault.

Based on the Tao Te Ching

MEDITATION

Into your hands, God, I commend my spirit.
(Silence)
Into your hands, God, I commend my spirit.

PRAYER

Christ, in your death you shared our sorrow
—In your resurrection you have given us hope.

Response: **Good Shepherd, hear our prayer.**

You humbled yourself to share our life. Make us generous in sharing our lives with all living creatures.

You are the way, the truth and the life. Fill us with the courage to always seek the truth in our lives.

By taking the lowest place, you gave life to all. Lead us to the peace of quiet loving service.

CLOSING

Jesus Christ, you have given your followers an example of gentleness and humility, a task that is

easy, a burden that is light. Accept the prayers and
work of this day, and give us the rest that will
strengthen us to render more faithful service to you.
—**Amen.**

The Liturgy of the Hours

BLESSING

Bless God, bless,
The whole Earth bless.

Quietly through the night,
Gently through the day,
Each and every creature
We meet upon our way.

Bless God, bless,
The whole Earth bless.

—**Amen.**

(Or)

May God the almighty, Mother and Father of us
all, give us rest tonight and peace at our death.
—**Amen.**

Winter Moon

OPENING

Awaken heart to what words cannot speak.
—**Moonlight upon the winter forest,**
  Snow upon the meadows,
  Silence—

What the heart cannot tell.

PSALM

Psalm of Winter Solitude

Antiphon: **Your name, O Lord, I cannot speak.**

Alone, I am alone,
  and in your darkness dance;
My feet creak upon the snow,
  my cheeks sting from your cold.

Jupiter blazes in this night.
The Moon grows brighter with the cloud
   passing in silence over my head
   and all is silent, all lies still.

Dark firs stand to my side,
   tall heads black against the sky.
Small tracks wander across my path,
   across the meadow white.

The land lies still
   under ten thousand fiery stars;
Earth lies cold and I stand still
And watch, my eyes and heart ablaze.

Antiphon: **Your name, O Lord, I cannot speak.**

MEDITATION

(Silence)

LITANY

   Softness of the powder snow
   Stillness of the winter frost

Rise of the distant summit
Chill of the mountain night
Light of the winter Moon
Purity of the untouched air
Cracking of the freezing ice
Silence of the land
Awe of my heart
Closing of my lips
Joy of my wonder

Oh, Lord, yes!
—Yes, my Lord!

(Bow or sign of worship)

PRAYER

A Prayer for Homo Sapiens

Source of all life,
For your name's sake,
For your joy cast upon the Earth,
For life's great delight in your handiwork,
Remember all the wounded and broken things,
    unclean water
    poisoned air

desecrated land
fleeing wildlife
dying innocents
And please remember us,
When our lives become enemies of your life,
Open our hearts to our family,
Earth's many children;
Return our hearts to you. Amen.

CLOSING

Our Father in heaven,
    hallowed be your name.
Your kingdom come.
Your will be done,
    on Earth as it is in heaven.

Matthew 6:9–10

—Amen.

BLESSING

I ask a blessing of my mother the Earth,
And of my father the Sun,
And of my sister the changing Moon,

And of my brother the unruly Air.

Most blessed are you, Almighty God!
I bow before you,
I wait and bow before you.

—Amen.

(Or)

Now may every living thing,
   young or old,
   weak or strong,
   living near or far,
   known or unknown,
   living or departed or yet unborn,
May every living thing,
   be full of bliss.

The Buddha

—Amen.

A Wider Universe

OPENING

LORD, you have been our dwelling place in all
generations.
—**Before the mountains were brought forth or
ever you had formed the Earth and the world,**

From everlasting to everlasting,
—**You are God.**

Psalm 90:1–2

PSALM

Hymn to Matter

Antiphon: **Blessed is the creation of God.**

Blessed be you, harsh, barren soil, stubborn rock:
you who yield only to violence,
you who force us to work if we would eat.

Blessed be you, perilous matter, violent sea,
    untameable passion:
you who unless we fetter you will devour us.

Blessed be you, mighty matter, irresistible
    march of evolution, reality ever newborn:
you who, by constantly shattering our mental
    categories, force us to go even further and
    further in our pursuit of the truth.

Blessed be you, universal matter,
    unmeasurable time, boundless ether,
    triple abyss of stars and atoms and generations:
you who by overflowing and dissolving our
    narrow standards of measurement
reveal to us the dimensions of God.

Antiphon: **Blessed is the creation of God.**

Pierre Teilhard de Chardin

FIRST READING

What struck me most was the silence. It was a great
silence, unlike any I have encountered on Earth, so
vast and deep that I began to hear my own body;
my heart beating, my blood vessels pulsing, even

the rustle of my muscles moving over each other seemed audible. There are more stars in the sky than I had expected. The sky was deep black, yet at the same time bright with sunlight. The Earth was small, light blue, and so touchingly alone, our home that must be defended like a holy relic. The Earth was absolutely round. I believe I never knew what the word round meant until I saw Earth from space.

Cosmonaut Aleksei Leonov

Second Reading

I talk about the Moon as being a very holy place.

Astronaut James Irwin

Third Reading

In the beginning when God created the heavens and the Earth, the Earth was a formless void and darkness covered the face of the deep while a wind from God swept over the face of the waters.

Genesis 1:1–2

MEDITATION

Welcome silence

(Silence)

Welcome silence

PRAYER

Oh, image of the invisible God, firstborn of all creation, grant us the courage to behold the fullness of God becoming manifest to our fearful eyes.

As you sweep back the boundaries of human knowledge
—Awaken us from our ignorance.

As human eyes behold a wider universe
—Open our hearts to wonder and fill our spirits with courage.

As the night of human misunderstanding dims
—Keep us watchful for the dawn we do not yet see.

As human awareness reunites with all creation
—Fill us with tender love for all creatures.

Closing

**Lead me from death to Life,
from falsehood to Truth**

**Lead me from despair
to Hope, from fear to Trust**

**Lead me from hate
to Love, from war to Peace**

**Let Peace fill our hearts,
our world, our universe.**

Satish Kumar

Blessing

God, infinite beyond our understanding, warm and
guide us, and all the small children of your great
Universe.
—Amen.

(Or)

May God the almighty, Mother and Father of us
all, give us rest tonight and peace at our death.
—Amen.

The Void

OO

OPENING

The voice of God speaks.
—Not even nothing can remain silent.

The voice of God silent.
—Listen.

(A moment of silence)

PSALM

Job 38:1–5, 6–7, 12, 31, 33, 36; 39:19–20, 26, 27

Antiphon: **I lay my hand upon my mouth.**

Job 40:4

Then the LORD answered Job
   out of the whirlwind:
"Who is this that darkens counsel
   by words without knowledge?
Gird up your loins like a man,

I will question you, and you shall declare
  to me.

"Where were you when I laid the foundation
   of the Earth?
Tell me if you have understanding.
Who determined its measurements—surely
   you know!

"Who laid its cornerstone
   when the morning stars sang together
and all the heavenly beings shouted for joy?

"Have you commanded the morning since your
   days began,
and caused the dawn to know its place?
Have the gates of death been revealed to you,
or have you seen the gates of deep darkness?

Can you bind the chains of the Pleiades,
   or loose the cords of Orion?
Do you know the ordinances of the heavens?
Can you establish their rule on the Earth?

Who has put wisdom in the inward parts,
   or given understanding to the mind?
Do you give the horse its might?
Do you clothe its neck with mane?
Do you make it leap like the locust?

Is it by your wisdom that the hawk soars,
and spreads its wings towards the south?
Is it at your command that the eagle mounts up
and makes it nest on high?

Antiphon: **I lay my hand upon my mouth.**

FIRST READING

The really terrifying thing about this life is that we do not understand it—not completely. No matter how normal reality may seem, no matter how many answers we've stored up in our libraries, we still have not the least idea of where reality originated from. God is the personification of our almost total and complete ignorance. The unnameable reality behind the terrible and awesome wonder of both life and this Universe, the reality behind our holiest and most sacred dreams, the reality behind everything dear and dreadful, this is the God we long to worship—even though we shall remain forever ignorant of God's totality in this life. Our minds are just too small. We shall be lucky to even see, like Moses, a glimpse of God's backside. And when we do, we'll probably think we've seen the whole of God.

SECOND READING

What, then, is the meaning of it all? What can we say to dispel the mystery of existence?

If we take everything into account—not only what the ancients knew, but all of what we know today that we didn't know—then I think we must frankly admit that *we do not know.*

Richard P. Feynman

MEDITATION

Be still

(Silence)

Be still

LITANY

Response: **From where do we come?**

Who gave us birth; who brought us forth . . . ?
Who gave us life; who gave us being . . . ?
Why can we ask; why can we know . . . ?
Listen to our voice . . .

Listen to our song . . .
Listen to our crying . . .
All of the Universe . . .
All of life before us . . .
All of life with us . . .
We speak . . .
We sing . . .

We die
—Lord, from where do we come?

PRAYER

O God, forgive us if we distrust you
—For every mystery we call by your name.

O God, forgive us if we fear you
—In every unknown we see your face.

Hidden God, thank you for courage, sustain us
in fear.
—Our hopes lie in you.

Thank you for fulfillment, sustain us in despair.
—Our hopes lie in you.

Thank you for enlightenment, sustain us in
doubt.
—Our hopes lie in you.

Thank you for beauty, sustain us in pollution.
—**Our hopes lie in you.**

CLOSING

God, sometimes hidden from our senses, our hearts take delight in the beauty of this life. We fear the terrors and speak angrily to you and each other of the things we cannot understand. May we hold fast to the quiet of peace, and trust in the long course of your work, reaching to a horizon far beyond us.
—**Amen.**

BLESSING

I did not ask,
   and yet a heart was given to me.

Of my origin I can only guess,
   but so real are my laughter when I laugh
   and my tears when I cry.

How deeply I am blessed.
How deeply I am blessed.

—Amen.

(Or)

Now may every living thing,
   young or old,
   weak or strong,
   living near or far,
   known or unknown,
   living or departed or yet unborn,
May every living thing,
   be full of bliss.

The Buddha

—Amen.

The Silent Sea

The LORD is my light and my salvation; whom
shall I fear?
—**The LORD is the stronghold of my life; of
whom shall I be afraid?**

Psalm 27:1–2

PSALM

Psalm 107:23–29

Antiphon: **Let God be praised for his wonderful works!**

Some went down to the sea in ships,
doing business on the mighty waters;
they saw the deeds of the LORD,
his wondrous works in the deep,
For he commanded and raised the stormy wind,
which lifted up the waves of the sea.

They mounted up to heaven, they went down to
    the depths;
  their courage melted away in their calamity;
they reeled and staggered like drunkards,
    and were at their wits' end.
Then they cried to the LORD in their trouble,
    and he brought them out from their distress;
he made the storm be still,
    and the waves of the sea were hushed.

Antiphon: **Let God be praised for his wonderful works!**

FIRST READING

The fair breeze blew, the white foam flew,
The furrow followed free;
We were the first that ever burst
Into that silent sea.

"The Rime of the Ancient Mariner"
Samuel Taylor Coleridge

SECOND READING

Every once in awhile we find ourselves out beyond
the bounds of metaphor and language where all is

strange, nothing is defined. In terror, we try to swim back to the safe shore of understanding. Next time, don't be so quick. The entire Universe is filled with this namelessness; all of known reality floats surrounded within and without by the unknown; that it should occasionally surround us is not unthinkable but inevitable, and are we put out there Adam-like for a purpose? Nothing known began that way. Every familiar landmark of the spirit and the Universe once was met by one courageous enough not to flee the namelessness.

THIRD READING

Immediately he made the disciples get into the boat and go on ahead to the other side, while he dismissed the crowds. And after he had dismissed the crowds, he went up the mountain by himself to pray. Then evening came, he was there alone, but by this time the boat, battered by the waves, was far from the land, for the wind was against them. And early in the morning he came walking toward them on the sea. But when the disciples saw him walking on the sea, they were terrified, saying, "It is a ghost!" And they cried out in fear. But immediately

Jesus spoke to them and said, "Take heart, it is I; do not be afraid."

Peter answered him, "Lord, if it is you, command me to come to you on the water." He said, "Come." So Peter got out of the boat, started walking on the water, and came toward Jesus. But when he noticed the strong wind, he became frightened and beginning to sink, he cried out, "Lord, save me!" Jesus immediately reached out his hand and caught him, saying to him, "You of little faith, why did you doubt?"

Matthew 14:22–31

MEDITATION

Let me not flee

(Silence)

Let me not flee

CLOSING

May the atmosphere we breathe
breathe fearlessness into us:

fearlessness on Earth
and fearlessness in Heaven!
May fearlessness guard us
behind and before!
May fearlessness surround us
above and below!
May we be without fear
of friend and foe!
May we be without fear
of the known and unknown!
May we be without fear
by night and by day!

The Vedas

—Amen.

BLESSING

Nameless God, awaken us to courage in this
    Universe.
May we never flee its unfamiliar face.
May we never fear the unexplained.
May we never deny the uncertain.

And bless us always with wisdom in the face of
the unknown.

—**Amen.**

(Or)

May God the almighty, Mother and Father of us
all, give us rest tonight and peace at our death.
—**Amen.**

Doubt

Within the night, within the silence
—**I wait for you, hidden God of the Universe.**

PSALM

Psalm of the Empty Night

Antiphon: **Your face is hidden, O God! How vast the empty night!**

The canyons slip down into darkness;
   my feet stumble beneath the stars.
No one lights my path or watches over my steps
   as parents watch after children,
     as the young are guided by elders.

In fear I turn unto you,
  and silence echoes:
  this night is so still and quiet.
All the words spoken to my heart
  have dried up;
My heart cannot remember joy.

I face this night alone.
If I return how shall I ever
  forget this darkness?
If I shall return,
  my joy has been swallowed in aloneness
  and I know that I stand between solitude and
    death.

Can the dawn bring any cheer
  if the night may soon swallow it?
Can the light bring any hope
  if the shadows overwhelm my soul?

My body is weary from the burden of this
    darkness,
  I fear sleep even as I fear this night.
I dare not abandon hope
  and yet how small my hope has become.

Antiphon: **Your face is hidden, O God! How vast the
empty night!**

READING

The scientist has a lot of experience with ignorance and doubt and uncertainty, and this experience is of very great importance, I think. When a scientist doesn't know the answer to a problem, he is ignorant. When he has a hunch as to what the result is, he is uncertain. And when he is pretty darn sure of what the result is going to be, he is still in some doubt. We have found it of paramount importance that in order to progress we must recognize our ignorance and leave room for doubt. Scientific knowledge—some most unsure, some nearly sure, but none *absolutely* certain.

Now, we scientists are used to this, and we take it for granted that it is perfectly consistent to be unsure, that it is possible to live and *not* know. But I don't know whether everyone realizes this is true. Our freedom to doubt was born out of a struggle against authority in the early days of science. It was a very deep and strong struggle: permit us to question—to doubt—to not be sure. I think that it is important that we do not forget this struggle and thus perhaps lose what we have gained. Herein lies a responsibility to society. . . .

It is our responsibility to leave the people of the future a free hand. In the impetuous youth of humanity, we can make grave errors that can stunt our growth for a long time. This we will do if we say we have the answers now, so young and ignorant as we are. If we suppress all discussion, all criticism, proclaiming "This is the answer, my friends; man is saved!" we will doom humanity for a long time to the chains of authority, confined to the limits of our present imagination. It has been done so many times before.

It is our responsibility as scientists, knowing the great progress which comes from a satisfactory philosophy of ignorance, the great progress which is the fruit of freedom of thought, to proclaim the value of this freedom; to teach how doubt is not to be feared but welcomed and discussed; and to demand this freedom as our duty to all coming generations.

Richard P. Feynman

MEDITATION

All shall be well
and all shall be well

**and all manner of thing
shall be well**

(Silence)

**All shall be well
and all shall be well
and all manner of thing
shall be well**

Julian of Norwich

Prayer

May those who doubt
—Trust in their doubt.

May those who cannot believe
—Trust in their disbelief.

May those who are tempted
—Trust their temptation.

May those who are alone
—Trust their aloneness.

May those who are abandoned
—Trust their abandonment.

May those who are desolate
—Trust their desolation.

For by this prayer alone
—All darkness is presented to you, O God.

And as you lead the lost so may you lead them
by means of that which they do not possess
—To that which they despair ever to find.

May your truth enlighten all paths
—And bring courage in all fears.

CLOSING

And yet, O God, would I find it any other way,
if you should send me out into the darkness?
You who have placed our souls out upon the
void,
watch over me.
I delight to trust in you:
I thank you for the adventure of unknowing
and fear!
I am honored that you have trusted me to
endure death
and the terror of ignorance!

—Amen.

BLESSING

Creator of all things, by your wisdom you have created doubt and discovery. Grant us courage and endurance in this life to accept ignorance and to seek truth. Speak to us tonight in our sleep and awaken us with the light of hope in the morning.
—**Amen.**

(Or)

May God the almighty, Mother and Father of us all, give us rest tonight and peace at our death.
—**Amen.**

All Shall Be Well

● ◐

Loving Mother, listen to the voices of this day
  inside my heart.
—**Open my eyes to see the eyes of your love.**

PSALM

Psalm 131

Antiphon: **Hope in the LORD, my soul.**

O LORD, my heart is not lifted up,
  my eyes are not raised too high;
I do not occupy myself with things
  too great and too marvelous for me.

But I have calmed and quieted my soul,
  like a weaned child with its mother;
My soul is like the weaned child that is with me.

O Israel, hope in the L ORD
    from this time on and forevermore.

Antiphon: **Hope in the L ORD, my soul.**

FIRST READING

Let nothing disturb you,
Nothing frighten you;
All things are passing;
God never changes,
Patient endurance
Attains all things;
Who possesses God
In nothing is wanting;
Alone God suffices.

Teresa of Avila

SECOND READING

All shall be well
    and all shall be well
    and all manner of thing
    shall be well.

Julian of Norwich

MEDITATION

Be still and know that I am God

(Silence)

Be still and know that I am God

PRAYER

Jesus, you promised to remain with us always,
even to the end of time.
—Please abide with us now.

When certainty eludes us
—Give us patience and trust.

When sin overwhelms those we love
—Hear the cries of our hearts.

When we are tempted
—May we hold fast to the light.

When evil threatens
—Enkindle good within us.

When the whole creation is filled with groaning
—Lord give answer.

And for the greatest cares of this day
—We turn now to you.

CLOSING

Like a mother you watch us, your children whom
you love. Comfort now our hearts for sleep, and
when we wake, may we rise in courage. We ask this
in the name of your Son, Jesus, the Christ.
—**Amen.**

BLESSING

Merciful God,
Loving Mother,
Guiding Light,
Let comfort come this night
for every wound and distress,
for every sorrow and uncertainty:
Your love shines upon us;
Your love will guard our rest.

—**Amen.**

(Or)

Now may every living thing,
young or old,
weak or strong,

living near or far,
known or unknown,
living or departed or yet unborn,
May every living thing,
be full of bliss.

The Buddha

—**Amen.**

Our Eyes Behold

God of all these wisdom and years,
—**Come and seek me out tonight.**

Psalm

Psalm of Wonder

Antiphon: **What do my eyes behold, O God?**

Once barren rock turned under storm
　　and became sand, but never soil.
And once waters bathed the Earth
　　and Sun warmed her, but no life came forth.

Until our eyes beheld, no one ever knew
　　that life endured unchanging
　　a billion upon a billion years,
And Cambrian life exploding

lay hidden in the stones
  until our eyes beheld and knew.

Triassic and Jurassic, O God,
  we have named ages,
Named miracles wrought unaware
  of their being or destiny,
  of our destiny within them.

Terrible lizards and life
  brought up to birth in death
  and agony:
Unknown, unheard, unseen across the Universe
  until our eyes saw.

The ages do not answer unto us;
From end to end, O God, where is life
  and the grand explosion of a Universe
    heading?
We are too small to know, and yet,
  O God, we behold.

Antiphon: **What do my eyes behold, O God?**

READING

I am the light that is over all things.
I am all:

all came forth from me,
and all attained to me.
Split a piece of wood,
and I am there.
Pick up a stone,
and you will find me there.

The Gospel of Thomas

MEDITATION

Be still

(Silence)

Be still

PRAYER

God of the Universe, let us not stop seeking
—**Until we find.**

When we find
—**Prepare our hearts to be disturbed by what we find.**
When we are disturbed
—**Lead us to amazement.**

And then, O God,
—**Lead us to rest. Amen.**

CLOSING

Dearest God, life has sustained itself through suffering; may we attain that deepest purpose for which we strive. And make gentle this night with your comfort.
—**Amen.**

BLESSING

With the gift of hope
   may God sustain us;
With the gift of love
   may we find God;
For the gift of life
   may we give thanks.

—**Amen.**

(Or)

May God the almighty, Mother and Father of us all, give us rest tonight and peace at our death.

—**Amen.**

Vision

● ◐

Behold! A sacred voice is calling you!
—All over the sky a sacred voice is calling!

Black Elk

PSALM

A Prayer of Black Elk

Antiphon: **Grandfather, Great Spirit, hear me! Listen to my voice calling you!**

Grandfather, Great Spirit, you have been always,
    and before you no one has been.
There is no other one to pray to but you.
You yourself, everything that you see,
    everything has been made by you.

The star nations all over the Universe you have
    finished.
The four quarters of the Earth you have finished.

The day, and in that day, everything you have
    finished.

Grandfather, Great Spirit, lean close to the Earth
    that you may hear the voice I send.
You towards where the Sun goes down, behold
    me;
    Thunder Beings, behold me!
You where the White Giant lives in power,
    behold me!

You where the Sun shines continually,
    whence come the day-break star and the day,
    behold me!
You where the summer lives, behold me!
You in the depths of the heavens,
    an eagle of power, behold!
And you, Mother Earth, the only Mother,
    you who have shown mercy to your children!

Hear me, four quarters of the world—relative I
    am!
Give me strength to walk the soft Earth,
    a relative to all that is!
Give me eyes to see and the strength to
    understand,
    that I may be like you.

With your power only can I face the winds.

Great Spirit, Great Spirit, my Grandfather,
　　all over the Earth the faces of living things are
　　　　all alike.
With tenderness have these come up out of the
　　ground.

Look upon these faces of children without
　　　　number
　　and with children in their arms,
　　　　that they may face the winds and walk the
　　　　　　good road to the day of quiet.
This is my prayer; hear me!
The voice I have sent is weak,
　　yet with earnestness I have sent it. Hear me!

Antiphon: **Grandfather, Great Spirit, hear me! Listen to
my voice calling you!**

FIRST READING

Then I was standing on the highest mountain of
them all, and round about beneath me was the
whole hoop of the world. And while I stood there I
saw more than I can tell and I understood more
than I saw; for I was seeing in a sacred manner the

shapes of all things in the spirit, and the shape of all shapes as they must live together like one being. And I saw that the sacred hoop of my people was one of many hoops that made one circle, wide as daylight and as starlight, and in the center grew one mighty flowering tree to shelter all the children of one mother and one father. And I saw that is was holy.

Black Elk

SECOND READING

The Six Grandfathers have placed in this world many things, all of which should be happy. Every little thing is sent for something, and in that thing there should be happiness and the power to make happy. Like the grasses showing tender faces to each other, thus we should do, for this was the wish of the Grandfathers of the World.

Black Elk

MEDITATION

In a sacred manner I am breathing
In a sacred manner I am quiet

(Silence)

In a sacred manner I am breathing
In a sacred manner I am quiet

PRAYER

Response: **Help us to seek the sacred way, Great Spirit.**

When we are a broken people . . .

When we no longer love either neighbor or stranger . . .

When we no longer include plants and animals in our family . . .

When we no longer love our children and teach them well . . .

When we no longer hope in visions and dreams . . .

When our understanding chills our love and ideals . . .

When we forget that the Earth is our Mother, the Universe our Father . . .

When life is no longer sacred . . .

When we are a broken planet . . .

Response: **Help us to seek the sacred way, Great Spirit.**

CLOSING

Grandfather, Great Spirit, behold us and lean to hear our feeble voice. You lived before us. All things belong to you, all living things. The good road and the road of difficulties you have made to cross; and where they cross, the place is holy. Day in and day out, forever, you are the life of things. You have said that we may approach you. Hear our prayers this night.
—**Amen.**

BLESSING

Great Spirit, behold us in kindness tonight. Grant us the day to be our companion, the night to be our comfort. May we walk in kindness with all

creatures, may your sacred way be found upon the Earth.
—**Amen.**

(Or)

Now may every living thing,
    young or old,
    weak or strong,
    living near or far,
    known or unknown,
    living or departed or yet unborn,
May every living thing,
    be full of bliss.

The Buddha

—**Amen.**

The Prayer of Our Wounded Ones

Dear God of Heaven and Earth,
—**Hear my voice this night.**

For all the mute and voiceless ones,
—**May I give voice to their prayers.**

PSALM

Psalm of Our Wounded Ones

Antiphon: **Spread wide, O God, your love upon the Earth.**

For the wounded lamb, the calf for slaughter,
  the dying chick, the misborn pup,
Hear their cries, O God, and for their world
    bring healing.

Let the dolphins prosper for your purpose,
 the seals find the plan you have ordered;
May the whales sing new songs of praise,
 the waves echo them to the heavens.

Quiet this Earth for all your children,
 restrain the human hand;
Bring rest to the weary and the ill;
Nourish and protect the endangered and the
  threatened.
Protect the weak for their own sake,
 even from our own hands protect them.

Remember, O God, the cats and all their
  descendants;
 remember each tree and every generation of
  seeds to come forth.
Grant to the meadows esteem in your sight;
Forget not the oceans and all that dwell therein.

Let not the small and the strange be swept away,
 till your voice has spoken through them.
Let not the useful and the vulnerable perish as
  our food,
 their heritage falling short of your delight.

THE PRAYER OF OUR WOUNDED ONES

Give ear to your creation, O God;
  for your name's sake deliver it;
And as your light is filling the heavens,
  may our hands turn back from evil
  and bring delight upon the Earth.

Antiphon: **Spread wide, O God, your love upon the Earth.**

READING

Recognize to whom you owe the fact that you exist,
that you breathe, that you understand, that you are
wise, and, above all, that you know God and hope
for the kingdom of heaven and the vision of glory,
now darkly and as in a mirror but then with greater
fullness and purity. You have been made a child of
God, coheir with Christ. Where did you get all this,
and from whom?

Let me turn to what is of less importance: the
visible world around us. What benefactor has en-
abled you to look out upon the beauty of the sky,
the Sun in its course, the circle of the Moon, the
countless number of stars, with the harmony and

order that are theirs, like the music of a harp? Who has blessed you with rain, with the art of husbandry, with different kinds of food, with the arts, with houses, with laws, with states, with a life of humanity and culture, with friendship and the easy familiarity of kinship?

Who has given you dominion over animals, those that are tame and those that provide you with food? Who has made you lord and master of everything on Earth? In short, who has endowed you with all that makes humans superior to all other living creatures?

Is it not God who asks you now in your turn to show yourself generous above all other creatures and for the sake of all other creatures? Because we have received from him so many wonderful gifts, will we not be ashamed to refuse him this one thing only, our generosity? Though he is God and Lord he is not afraid to be known as our Father. Shall we for our part repudiate those who are our kith and kin?

Let us put into practice the supreme and primary law of God. He sends down rain on just and sinful alike, and causes the Sun to rise on all without distinction. To all Earth's creatures he has given the broad Earth, the springs, the rivers and forests. He has given the air to the birds, and the waters to those who live in water. He has given abundantly to all the basic needs of life, not as a private possession, not restricted by law, not divided by boundaries, but as common to all, amply and in rich measure. His gifts are not deficient in any way, because he wanted to give equality of blessing to equality of worth, and to show the abundance of his generosity.

Gregory of Nazianzen

MEDITATION

May my heart be open

(Silence)

May my heart be open

LITANY

Response: **I sing your praise!**

> Together with all creation . . .
> With the Sun and Moon . . .
> With the wind and air . . .

With the rivers and oceans . . .
With the hills and meadows . . .
With the grass and flowers . . .
With the elk and lion . . .
With the ant and spider . . .
With the dolphin and fish . . .
With the sparrow and eagle . . .
With all the Earth and all the Universe . . .

GREAT BLESSING

Now may every living thing,
   young or old,
   weak or strong,
   living near or far,
   known or unknown,
   living or departed or yet unborn,
May every living thing,
   be full of bliss

The Buddha

PRAYER

Instruction: Pause and call to mind the wounded
and broken plants and animals that live near to you

and especially the wild and endangered ones that few people see and care for. Hold them in gentle silence inside your heart before the love of their Creator. (A group may wish to name the creatures aloud and then pause in silence after each.)

BLESSING

Blessing of the Senses*

> In my eyes blessing
> In my hearing blessing
> In my lips blessing
> In my touch blessing
> In my smelling blessing
> In my mind blessing
> May my life bring blessing to the Earth

> **—Amen.**

* SACRED SIGN FOR BLESSING
(To anoint oneself for the above blessing: both hands together touch the eyes, the ears, the lips, come together palm to palm for touch, touch the nose, touch the head, palms to the top of the head; then for life the arms cross the chest and for bringing blessing to the Earth the arms open wide. To anoint another, change the pronoun to "your" and as you recite, with your

(Or)

  Now may every living thing,
      young or old,
      weak or strong,
      living near or far,
      known or unknown,
      living or departed or yet unborn,
  May every living thing,
      be full of bliss.

The Buddha

—**Amen.**

hands gently touch their eyes, ears, lips, hold their hands, gently touch their noses, rest upon their heads then for "life" lay your hands upon their shoulders, and for bringing blessing to the Earth open your arms wide in front of them. Next, the other anoints you and the blessing is ended by sharing some sign of peace.)

The Stones Would Shout Out!

OPENING

> O Lord, open my lips,
> **—And my mouth will proclaim your praise.**
>
> *Psalm 51:15*

PSALM

Psalm of the Stones

Antiphon: **Our voice is the voice of stones, singing your praise!**

> O God, how have we been given such eyes
>   that we should look beyond our birth?
> How have we been given such lips
>   that we should tell of eternities before us?
>
> Before your eyes, the humble stones lay so long,
>   that my life upon them,

Is but a passing shadow,
 the flicker of a wing in flight.

Long lay the rocks and ages, silent before you;
From death to death, unknowing but known.
Within rivers you conceived me,
 within death you sow your seed;
Wondrous the death of rocks that gave me birth!

O wonder, that stone ever gave birth!
Mountains pass to sand,
 the sand to dust,
And from the dust we have been formed.

Antiphon: **Our voice is the voice of stones, singing your praise!**

FIRST READING

The rocks are not so close akin to us as the soil; they are one more remove from us; but they lie back of all . . . Rocks have literally come down to us from a foreworld. The youth of the Earth is in the soil and in the trees and verdure that spring from it; its age is in the rocks.

John Burroughs

SECOND READING

As he was now approaching the path down from the Mount of Olives, the whole multitude of the disciples began to praise God joyfully with a loud voice for all the deeds of power that they had seen, saying,

> Blessed is the king
>   who comes in the name of the Lord!
> Peace in heaven
>   and glory in the highest heaven!

Some of the Pharisees in the crowd said to him, "Teacher, order your disciples to stop." He answered, "I tell you, if these were silent, the stones would shout out."

Luke 19:37–40

MEDITATION

God has called me forth

(Silence)

God has called me forth

LITANY

Response: **The stones themselves would still praise you.**

Had it not been our own voice . . .
Had it not been our parents' voice . . .
Had it not been a human voice . . .
Had it not been a mammal voice . . .
Had it not been a living voice . . .
Had it not been stars and galaxies . . .
Had it not been this Universe . . .

But rejoice, and let us tonight sing!
—The heavens are telling the glory of God!

Our eyes behold the wonders God has done!
—And our lips are proclaiming his praise!

PRAYER

Today is the acceptable time!
—This, today, is the day of salvation!

God, let not our hands destroy
—What your love has created.

Let not our hearts despise
—Anything your hand has made.

Let not our eyes turn away from
—The least of your creatures.

CLOSING

Make of us new vessels, fill us with new loves,
awaken us to your glory, for this day we have been
called to understand the work of your hands. The
crisis of this age is the moment of history to which
you have brought us; Earth groans and the heavens
await the birth of the children of God, who are
given the high privilege and great calling of loving
all things as they have been loved. Today is the
acceptable time!
—This, today, is the day of salvation!

BLESSING

May the one who has begun a good work in us bring
it to completion.

Based on Philippians 1:6

—**Amen.**

(Or)

May God the almighty, Mother and Father of us
all, give us rest tonight and peace at our death.
—**Amen.**

A Wider Circle

OPENING

In your presence, my brothers and sisters, my
mothers and fathers—all living creatures—
—I come tonight.

PSALM

Not Man Apart

Antiphon: **It is only a little planet, but how beautiful it is.**

It is only a little planet
But how beautiful it is.
Water that owns the north and west and south

And all is colors and never is all quiet,
And the fogs are its breath . . .

All the free companies of windy grasses . . .
pure naked rock . . .

A lonely clearing;
   a little field of corn by the streamside;
   a roof under sparred trees.
Love that, not man apart from that . . .

Robinson Jeffers

Antiphon: **It is only a little planet, but how beautiful it is.**

First Reading

All ethics so far evolved rest upon a single premise: that the individual is a member of a community of interdependent parts. His instincts prompt him to compete for his place in the community, but his ethics prompt him also to cooperate (perhaps in order that there may be a place to compete for).

The land ethic simply enlarges the boundaries of the community to include soils, waters, plants, and animals, or collectively: the land. . . .

In short, a land ethic changes the role of *Homo sapiens* from a conqueror of the land-community to plain member and citizen of it. It implies respect for his fellow-members, and also respect for the community as such.

Aldo Leopold

SECOND READING

Something is lacking and because of that lack education, law and public works fail to accomplish what they hope to accomplish. Without that something, the high-minded impulse to educate, to legislate and to manage become as sounding brass and tinkling cymbals. And the thing which is missing is love, some feeling for, as well as some understanding of, the inclusive community of rocks and soils, plants and animals, of which we are a part.

Joseph Wood Krutch

THIRD READING

A human being is part of the whole, called by us the Universe. A part limited in time and space. He experiences himself, his thoughts and feelings, as something separate from the rest, a kind of optical delusion of his consciousness. This delusion is a kind of prison for us, restricting us to our personal desires and to affection for a few persons nearest to us. Our task must be to free ourselves from this prison by widening our circle of compassion to embrace all living creatures.

Albert Einstein

MEDITATION

I open my heart to all of life with me

(Silence)

May all of life be blessed

LITANY

Response: **Let us pray.**

For the birds of the air . . .
For the fish and all that dwell in water . . .
For our own family of mammals . . .
For insects and spiders . . .
For all creatures too small to be seen . . .
For the meadows and forests . . .
For the deserts and tundras . . .
For the rivers and oceans . . .
For all that has life and breath . . .

Come Great Spirit
—And renew the face of the Earth!

PRAYER

We pray for all people
—Great Spirit send us rain and crops for food.

We pray for all people
**—Great Spirit send us health and a path of light
at death.**

We pray for all animals
**—Great Spirit may our brothers and sisters find
food and homes.**

We pray for all animals
**—Great Spirit may our brothers and sisters find
the hidden paths by which you lead them.**

We pray for all plants
**—Great Spirit may our mothers and fathers
find good soil and abundant rain.**

We pray for all plants
**—Great Spirit may our mothers and fathers
find in us virtue and respect equal to their gifts.**

CLOSING

Spirit of God, may our hearts always love the Earth.
May we love the land and the sky and the water.

May our hands touch in reverence and our feet walk with respect upon the Earth. Many gifts you give; may our eyes behold them when we wake tomorrow.

—**Amen.**

BLESSING

Bright be the breeze of childhood;
Bright be childhood's ending;
Bright be the dawn on our understanding;
Bright be the shining forth of light.
Unto every creature you send us,
May our path come as light;
Unto every door that opens,
May enlightenment enter.

—**Amen.**

(Or)

Now may every living thing,
    young or old,
    weak or strong,
    living near or far,

known or unknown,
   living or departed or yet unborn,
May every living thing,
   be full of bliss.

The Buddha

—Amen.

Repentance

OPENING

Create in me a clean heart, O God,
—**And put a new and right spirit within me.**

Restore to me the joy of your salvation,
—**And sustain in me a willing spirit.**

O Lord, open my lips,
—**And my mouth will declare your praise.**

Psalm 51:10, 12, 15

PSALM

Psalm of the Open Heart

Antiphon: **God of my life, lead me to truth.**

Out of your hands, you have given every thing
for life, O God;
out of your love, every being has been called
forth.

O God, even if you had not written a word,
   your word is woven in the fabric of your works.
We can pretend and hide and dodge each other,
   using laws and commandments to thwart our
      foes,
But we cannot hide from you, for your
      commandments
   are so knit within our being
That to violate them we must necessarily
   violate our own selves.

And yet you have not made us mindless
      elements,
   mere machines to obey and never choose;
Indeed, you have so crafted our souls,
   that if we do not choose we cannot remain
   righteous before you.

You are a hard master,
   expecting to reap where you have not sown;
You expect of us the harvest of our own souls,
   and though we cry out for aid,
   you will never send one to take our place.

No matter where we hear your voice,
   you call us to heed it.
If we call your voice the voice of an enemy
   then we call you an enemy.

Make wise our ears, open our hearts,
No matter what wisdom we have before received
   let not our understanding of it
   blind us to your truth.
O God, keep us from the great sorrow
   of missing your presence among us,
   disguised as sheep in wolves' clothing.

Antiphon: **God of my life, lead me to truth.**

FIRST READING

To end environmental abuse you must put an end
to environmental abuse inside of yourself. How
easy it is for people to agree with this and still do
nothing; and if they do nothing, their agreement
means nothing. To call yourself an environmentalist and do nothing is to compound the Earth's woes.
To call yourself an environmentalist and wait for
others to change the human relationship with the
Earth is to betray the Earth. Each and every human
is accountable for their treatment of the Earth because they have all received from the Earth their life
and owe to it their existence. In the presence of God
who gave you life through the Earth, her life sys-

tems must become your first loyalty, not your last, for you know of no greater creature your God has made or loved.

SECOND READING

Why do you call me "Lord, Lord," and do not do what I tell you? I will show you what someone is like who comes to me, hears my words, and acts on them. That one is like a man building a house, who dug deeply and laid the foundation on rock; when a flood arose, the river burst against that house but could not shake it, because it had been well built. But the one who hears and does not act is like a man who built a house on the ground without a foundation. When the river burst against it, immediately it fell, and great was the ruin of that house.

Luke 6:46–49

MEDITATION

**How shall I live my life
full of compassion and truth?**

(Silence)

**How shall I live my life
full of compassion and truth?**

LITANY

Response: **Let me live my life and choose my actions.**

As a friend of the Great Spirit . . .
As a friend of the Earth . . .
As a friend of the atmosphere . . .
As a friend to the waters . . .
As a friend to the land . . .
As a friend to every living thing . . .
As a friend of the Great Spirit . . .

PRAYER

Eternal God of love, you have sent the rain and the sunshine upon us all. Even if we should turn away from you, your love will not end. All of us have sinned and fallen short. All of us have acted in ignorance and abuse of the source of our lives. Let not

Welcome dirt and stone . . .
Welcome life among us . . .

Come Holy Spirit
—And renew the face of the Earth.

PRAYER

Lord Jesus, you humbled yourself to come down
among us. Lord Christ, you humbled yourself to
become the Word of our creation.
—Awaken us this spring.

As new life returns to your land,
—Awaken joy within our hearts.

As the changing season disorients us,
—Open our hearts to new life.

For those handicapped and disabled,
—May we quietly serve them.

For those who fall in love,
—May they discover bliss.

For those of us who ignorantly or willfully act as
enemies of life and the living creatures,
—Teach us your love in every creature.

CLOSING

Lord, fill this night with your radiance
May we sleep in peace and rise with joy
To greet the light of a new day in your name.
—**Amen.**

The Liturgy of the Hours

BLESSING

Lord of Life, come and bless us this night, renew
our world as we sleep and unite us with you at
our death.
—**Amen.**

(Or)

Now may every living thing,
    young or old,
    weak or strong,
    living near or far,
    known or unknown,
    living or departed or yet unborn,
May every living thing,
    be full of bliss.

The Buddha

—**Amen.**

Desert

Lord, I think of you on my bed,
**—And meditate on you in the watches of the
night.**

Psalm 63:6

PSALM

Desert Psalm

Antiphon: **O God, you are from everlasting.**

The deserts know your voice
   in the winds and the rains.
Barren rocks and barren planets
   all have come from your hand!

The coyotes lift up their song,
   into the night they sing,
You have given them voice
   and with your voice they sing.

The mountains stand in silence;
   the canyons hold the darkness.
Frogs delight in hidden springs;
   the birds have taken their rest.

Life has filled your deserts,
   they echo, the caverns echo
   with song:
Cliffrose and sagebrush swell
   with sweet fragrance,
As rain fills the canyons
   with torrents.

Stars sparkle in darkness,
   moonlight wakens the night;
Silently the owl glides.
Within this sacred night,
   within this sacred land,
I look to you, O Lord.

Antiphon: **O God, you are from everlasting.**

READING

Are not five sparrows sold for two pennies?
Yet not one of them is forgotten in God's sight.

Luke 12:6

MEDITATION

Open heart. Be still

(Silence)

Open heart. Be still

LITANY

Holy Spirit,
Barren rock and wandering dunes
—Delight in your love

Cactus blossom and rattlesnake
—Delight in your love

Dry heat and dust devil
—Delight in your love

Canyon and mesa
—Delight in your love

Pinyon and juniper
—Delight in your love

Scorpion and coyote
—Delight in your love

Come Holy Spirit
—Open our eyes

Come Holy Spirit
—Silence our fears

Come Holy Spirit
—Open our hearts

Come Holy Spirit
—Let us delight in your love

PRAYER

Father of Life, this night is full of wonder;
Mother of Life, this night is full of joy.
—May we take delight in your love.

Response: **Great Creator, hear us.**

As at the desert springs, may all find healing and rest.

As in the desert canyons, may all paths lead to delight.

As on the high mesas, may all draw close to you.

As in the desert night, may all be full of peace.

CLOSING

A Prayer of Seven Directions*

With beauty before me,
  May I walk
With beauty behind me,
  May I walk
With beauty on my right,
  May I walk
With beauty on my left,
  May I walk
With beauty above me,
  May I walk
With beauty below me,
  May I walk
With beauty inside me,
  May I walk
Wandering on a trail of beauty,
  Lively, I walk

Adapted from a Navajo prayer

* Optional hand motions for this prayer: BEFORE—arms
stretch forward, palms face forward, BEHIND—arms pull
back, palms face backwards either at hips (if standing) or
shoulders (if sitting), RIGHT—extend right arm with palm up
and hold, LEFT—extend left arm with palm up and hold,

BLESSING

God of the wind, sand and stars
God of the planets drifting in silence
May all eyes be blessed to behold your glory
    forever.
How delightful the day and the night!
May we always delight in you.

—**Amen.**

(Or)

Now may every living thing,
    young or old,
    weak or strong,
    living near or far,
    known or unknown,
    living or departed or yet unborn,
May every living thing,
    be full of bliss.

The Buddha

—**Amen.**

ABOVE—keeping arms extended, raise palms upwards, BELOW—turn palms down and lower arms, INSIDE—bring fingertips to the center of your chest, WANDERING—open hands like a blossom out from chest until arms extend to left and right, palms facing up.

The Mountain

Within this sacred night, within this sacred land,
—**I look to you, O Lord.**

PSALM

Psalm of the Mountains

Antiphon: **May my eyes behold, O God!**

The mountains rise from the plains;
  all the land lies low beneath them.
The winds race across the summits;
  summer snows frost the tundra slopes.

Deep rivers run down through the canyons
  cutting past the mangled layers of melted
    stone,
The firs and spruce gather darkly upon the slopes
  while the aspens approach the bright
    meadows.

Rosy granites disintegrate to pink gravel
    under the open forest of giant ponderosa pine;
Brown blankets of long needles lie at their base.
    Jays call from the scrub oaks.

The cool breeze makes the dark blue lake
      sparkle in the sunlight;
The wind sighs in the needles as the fish move
    in the cold waters.

Mountain goats move freely without shepherds,
    elk thunder across the meadows,
The bear and her cub pass by the stream willows,
    an eagle glides out across the dark canyon.

The mountains rise from the plains,
    the waves of continents crashing.
The mountains rise from the Earth,
    out into the empty sky they rise;
At night the mountains stand out in the cold
    that wraps the distant stars.

Antiphon: **May my eyes behold, O God!**

FIRST READING

No landscape is discovered from the mountaintop,
if you have not struggled up the slopes; for the land-

scape is not a mere sight but something achieved and conquered. If you have yourself carried to the summit in a litter, you still see but a more or less uninspiring pattern, and how will you add savor to it from within yourself?

Antoine de Saint Exupery

SECOND READING

No matter where your interest lies, you will not be able to accomplish anything unless you bring your deepest devotion to it.

Basho

THIRD READING

I climbed Mount Gassan on the eighth . . . I walked through mists and clouds, breathing the thin air of high altitudes and stepping on slippery ice and snow, till at last through a gateway of clouds, as it seemed, to the very paths of the Sun and Moon, I reached the summit, completely out of breath and nearly frozen to death. Presently the Sun went

down and the Moon rose glistening in the sky. I
spread some leaves on the ground and went to
sleep, resting my head on pliant bamboo branches.
When, on the following morning, the Sun rose
again and dispersed the clouds, I went down towards Mount Yudono . . .

When I returned . . . I wrote as follows.

How cool it is,
A pale crescent shining
Above the dark hollow
Of Mount Haguro.

How many columns of clouds
Had risen and crumbled, I wonder
Before the silent Moon rose
Over Mount Gassan.

Forbidden to betray
The holy secrets of Mount Yudono,
I drenched my sleeves in reticent tears.

Tears rushed to my eyes
As I stepped knowingly
Upon the coins on the sacred road
Of Mount Yudono.

Basho

FOURTH READING

Though I be suffering and weak, and all
My youthful spring be gone, yet have I come
Leaning upon my staff, clambered up
The mountain peak.

          My cloak thrown off,
My little bowl o'erturned, so sit I here
Upon the rock. And o'er my spirit sweeps
The breath of liberty! 'Tis won, 'tis won,
The triple Lore! The Buddha's will is done!

Theragatha, Psalm 24, Pali Canon

MEDITATION

Instruction: If a mountain, hill or mesa is visible,
you may wish to turn and face toward it

**Beholding the magnificence of that which is I am at
peace and silent**

(Silence)

**Beholding the magnificence of that which is I am at
peace and silent**

PRAYER

Instruction: Speak to God softly of the concerns of
your heart.

CLOSING

Quiet the land, O Maker of the land
Quiet my heart, O Maker of my heart
As you have made the Earth majestic
May my heart sing of your majesty
As you have made all things to grow
May I grow unto your stature
That after the final night
I will awaken into your presence

—Amen.

BLESSING

Send, O God, a blessing upon the mountains
    and upon the distant shores.
Send, O God, a blessing upon all of us
    who live small upon this planet.

And send, O God, a blessing
   upon all who see no blessing's hope.

—**Amen.**

(Or)

May God the almighty, Mother and Father of us
all, give us rest tonight and peace at our death.

—**Amen.**

Earth and Heaven Speak

Heaven and Earth speak of God's glory
—**Let all creation echo in praise!**

PSALM

Psalm of the Heavens

Antiphon: **How wonderful are your heavens, O God!**

Vast the heavens, stars and quasars,
  galaxies and nebula:
From the chaos of atoms
  the stones upon which we stand
  have been created;
From the chaos of the Earth and the Sun
  our lives have been ordered.

Earth turns in and out of darkness,
   the creatures of night and day keeping watch.
Puma and deer approach the flow of springs
    hidden within the layers of rock;

Cottonwoods and grasses, sages and roses
   mingle with sand and stone,
   mesa and stream;
Within these the rabbits and birds take refuge.

Frogs, snakes and flocks of birds
   make their homes within the wetlands;
Nighthawks and bats,
   gnats and mosquitoes
   feed in the dusk,
And the owl and the moth
   move hidden through the night.

The grasses of the prairies
   feed life in great abundance,
Dark forests and high mountains
   hold the cool airs and snows.
From the poles the winter descends
   and from the equator swells the summer.
Rainforests mingle abundance precariously;
   upon ice sheets microbes find a home.

Earth, beside the Sun is a shelter for life,
   a dwelling of great delight,
And the wide sea of the Universe
   bears us inside.

Antiphon: **How wonderful are your heavens, O God!**

FIRST READING

Sons and daughters of the Earth, steep yourselves in the sea of matter, bathe in its fiery waters, for it is the source of your life and your youthfulness.

You thought you could do without it because the power of thought has been kindled in you? You hoped that the more thoroughly you rejected the tangible, the closer you would be to spirit: that you would be more divine if you lived in the world of pure thought, or at least more angelic if you fled the corporeal? Well, you were like to have perished of hunger.

You must have oil for your limbs, blood for your veins, water for your soul, the world of reality for your intellect: do you not see that the very law of your nature makes these a necessity for you?

Pierre Teilhard de Chardin

SECOND READING

Why do we have such a wonderful idea of God? Because we live in such a gorgeous world. We wonder at the magnificence of whatever it is that brought the world into being. This leads to a sense of adoration. We have a sense of immense gratitude that we participate in such a beautiful world. This adoration, this gratitude, we call religion. Now, however, as the outer world is diminished, our inner world is dried up.

If we lived on the Moon, for example, our sense of the divine would reflect the lunar landscape. We would not have anything like the awareness of the divine that we have at present. Imagination is required for religious development. What would there be to imagine if we lived on the Moon? We would have something, but it would be very meagre. Our sensitivities would be dull because our inner world would reflect the outer world. Intelligence would be so stunted that it would be hardly developed at all. Why? Because there would be very little to name, very little to discuss or to talk about. There would still be the great question of existence and nonexistence, so perhaps human intelligence would have some development. We would have some inner life. But think of being born on the Moon and then coming to the Earth. What a stunning beatific experience that would be!

In reverse, if we lived on the Earth and then put ourselves back on the Moon, what would we be missing? We would be moving from a sense of existence, a sense of the human, a sense of the beauty in a creative world, back to an extinction of everything that we have here. For religion not to realize that, not to safeguard the basis of its own survival, for humans not to appreciate the source of their arts, their science, their dance, their whole intellectual and affective life, their whole expansiveness of soul and mind and heart, and not to feel that endangered by what we are doing to ourselves: how strange!

Thomas Berry

MEDITATION

(Silence)

PRAYER

Almighty God, tonight hear our prayer!

Let us make known among the nations
—The wonders of the heavens and the Earth.

Let us honor in our words and deeds
—The Creator of all the Universe.

Let our hearts and hands
—Take care for every creature.

Let us treasure the honor
—Of our high position upon the Earth, of our vision to the distant planets and stars, of our ability to watch the atoms and microbes.

And let us take care for the truth
—And seek it well without prejudice or fear,

For our trust is in the God who created us;
—His works testify to his love and compassion.

And in God
—We take great delight this night.

CLOSING

Enlighten our understanding
Console our pain

Guide us in the small things
Give us delight
Give us rest and in the morning
Lead us to joy

—**Amen.**

Blessing

May almighty God bless us, beyond all things,
walking beside us and deep within forever.
—**Amen.**

(Or)

Now may every living thing,
   young or old,
   weak or strong,
   living near or far,
   known or unknown,
   living or departed or yet unborn,
May every living thing,
   be full of bliss.

The Buddha

—**Amen.**

In the Presence
of My Enemies

● ◐

OPENING

God, come to my assistance!
—**Lord make haste to help me!**

The Liturgy of the Hours

PSALM

Psalm 3

Antiphon: **Rise up, O LORD! Deliver me, O my God!**

O LORD, how many are my foes!
  Many are rising against me;
many are saying to me,
  "There is no help for you in God."

But you, O LORD, are a shield around me,
  my glory, and the one who lifts up my head.

I cry aloud to the Lord,
   and he answers me from his holy hill.

I lie down and sleep;
   I wake again, for the Lord sustains me.
I am not afraid of ten thousands of people
   who have set themselves against me all
     around.

Rise up, O Lord!
   Deliver me, O my God!
For you strike all my enemies on the cheek;
   you break the teeth of the wicked.

Deliverance belongs to the Lord;
   may your blessing be on your people!

Antiphon: **Rise up, O Lord! Deliver me, O my God!**

First Reading

In our anger we wish for the teeth of the wicked to
be broken, just as we might strike the wall against
which we stubbed our toe. But it is not the wicked
or the wall which must be broken, it is evil. We
cannot confront evil with evil thoughts in our
hearts. We will accomplish nothing good. Love

your enemies. Look at them and at yourself with gentleness and compassion. Seek understanding. Pray for reconciliation with your opponent even as you pray for wisdom and courage in confronting evil. Believe that good will triumph and master your fears.

SECOND READING

You have heard that it was said, "You shall love your neighbor and hate your enemy." But I say to you, Love your enemies and pray for those who persecute you, so that you may be children of your Father in heaven; for he makes his Sun rise on the evil and on the good, and sends rain on the righteous and on the unrighteous.

Matthew 5:43–45

MEDITATION

Be still my soul within me

(Silence)

Be still my soul within me

PRAYER

Brother Jesus, in your betrayal and death, you share our worst betrayal and maddening defeat.
—Lead us through death to life.

Response: **Father, into your hands I commend my spirit.**

Through seasons of trial and darkness keep my heart open to the beauty of all creatures.

Make me wise to understand my enemies, and compassionate to their pain.

Let not my enemies control me through anger, bitterness or fear.

Grant me rest of body and mind, and a quiet spirit within.

CLOSING

**Lead me from death to Life,
from falsehood to Truth**

**Lead me from despair
to Hope, from fear to Trust**

**Lead me from hate
to Love, from war to Peace**

**Let Peace fill our heart,
our world, our universe.**

Satish Kumar

BLESSING

Come, abide the night with us, Holy Spirit; and
help us walk tomorrow's path.
—**Amen.**

(Or)

May God the almighty, Mother and Father of us
all, give us rest tonight and peace at our death.
—**Amen.**

A Bruised Reed

● ◑

I bless the LORD who gives me counsel;
in the night also my heart instructs me.
—I keep the LORD always before me.

Psalm 16:7–8

PSALM

Psalm 19

Antiphon: **May the glory of the LORD endure forever;
may the LORD rejoice in his works.**

Psalm 104:31

The heavens are telling the glory of God;
and the firmament proclaims his handiwork.
Day to day pours forth speech,
and night to night declares knowledge.

There is no speech, nor are there words;
   their voice is not heard;
yet their voice goes out through all the Earth,
   and their words to the end of the world.

In the heavens he has set a tent for the Sun,
which comes out like a bridegroom from his
      wedding canopy,
   and like a strong man runs its course with joy.
Its rising is from the end of the heavens,
   and its circuit to the end of them;
   and nothing is hid from its heat.

The law of the LORD is perfect,
   reviving the soul;
the decrees of the LORD are sure,
   making wise the simple;
the precepts of the LORD are right,
   rejoicing the heart;
the commandment of the LORD is clear,
   enlightening the eyes;
the fear of the LORD is pure,
   enduring forever;
the ordinances of the LORD are true
   and righteous altogether.
More to be desired are they than gold,

even much fine gold,
sweeter also than honey,
     and drippings of the honeycomb.

Moreover by them is your servant warned;
     in keeping them there is great reward.
But who can detect their errors?
     Clear me from hidden faults.
Keep back your servant also from the insolent;
     do not let them have dominion over me.
Then I shall be blameless,
     and innocent of great transgression.

Let the words of my mouth and the meditation
     of my heart
be acceptable to you,
O LORD, my rock and my redeemer.

Antiphon: **May the glory of the LORD endure forever;
may the LORD rejoice in his works.**

FIRST READING

Here is my servant, whom I uphold,
     my chosen, in whom my soul delights;

I have put my spirit upon him;
    he will bring forth justice to the nations.
He will not cry or lift up his voice,
    or make it heard in the street;
a bruised reed he will not break,
    and a dimly burning wick he will not quench;
    he will faithfully bring forth justice.
He will not grow faint or be crushed
    until he has established justice in the Earth;
    and the coastlands wait for his teaching.

Isaiah 42:1–4

SECOND READING

It is said that in the last few years, two million square miles of forest land have been destroyed by acid rain, and that is partly because of our cars. "Before starting the car, I know where I am going," is a very deep question. "Where shall I go? To my own destruction?" If trees die, humans are going to die also. If trees and animals are not alive, how can we be alive?

"The car and I are one." We have the impression that we are the boss, and the car is only an instrument, but that is not true. With the car, we become something different. With a gun, we become very dangerous. With a flute, we become pleasant. With 50,000 atomic bombs, humankind has become the most dangerous species on Earth. We were never so dangerous as we are now. We should be aware. The most basic precept of all is to be aware of what we do, what we are, each minute. Every other precept will follow from that.

Thich Nhat Hanh

MEDITATION

What are the things, beyond my own species that I love?

(Meditate in silence)

How do my actions harm these things that I love?

(Meditate in silence)

Where is the way of turning to actions of deeper love?

(With gentle love for yourself and the objects of your love, quietly search for a compassionate way to heal. If no way appears, then quietly hold yourself and your loves before the compassion of God.)

PRAYER

This day,
—May my feet bring blessing to the land.

(Pause after each petition)

This day,
—May my hands bring blessing to the waters.

This day,
—May my breath bring blessing to the air.

This day,
—May my thoughts bring blessing to all of life.

This day,
—May I be aware of the whole.

This day,
—May I be aware of the forgotten.

This day,
—May I be aware of my loves.

This day,
—May my life bring bliss to the Earth.

CLOSING

**Lead me from death to Life,
from falsehood to Truth**

**Lead me from despair
to Hope, from fear to Trust**

**Lead me from hate
to Love, from war to Peace**

**Let Peace fill our heart,
our world, our Universe.**

Satish Kumar

BLESSING

A blessing God upon the flesh of the Earth that
I have bruised needlessly.
A blessing God upon the spirits of the living
things I have harmed needlessly.
A blessing God upon myself that I might
become aware not unto guilt but unto
compassion for that All of which I am a part.

—Amen.

(Or)

Now may every living thing,
young or old,
weak or strong,

living near or far,
known or unknown,
living or departed or yet unborn,
May every living thing,
be full of bliss.

The Buddha

—Amen.

Compassion

Though we dread to speak,
—**Let our lips open;**

Perchance we shall find
—**Light where all lies now in darkness.**

PSALM

Psalm 130

Antiphon: **Out of the depths I cry to you, O LORD!**

Out of the depths I cry to you, O LORD.
  Lord, hear my voice!
Let your ears be attentive
  to the voice of my supplications!

If you, O LORD, should mark iniquities,
  Lord, who could stand?

But there is forgiveness with you,
   so that you may be revered.

I wait for the LORD, my soul waits,
   and in his word I hope;
my soul waits for the Lord
   more than those that watch for the morning,
   more than those that watch for the morning.

O Israel, hope in the LORD!
   For with the LORD there is steadfast love,
   and with him is great power to redeem.
It is he who will redeem Israel
   from all its iniquities.

Antiphon: **Out of the depths I cry to you, O LORD!**

FIRST READING

Some politicians came, and to test Jesus they asked him, "Is it lawful for a woman to have an abortion?" He answered them, "What does the law state?" They said, "The Supreme Court has allowed a woman to have an abortion." But Jesus said to them, "Because of the hardness of human hearts this has been done. But from the beginning of creation, 'God made them male and female.' For this reason a man shall leave his father and mother and be joined to a woman, and the two shall become one flesh."

Then one of the politicians objected, "Not only have you given that same answer for the question of divorce, but you haven't answered the question of abortion in cases of rape and incest and when the mother's life is endangered, either psychologically or physically."

"But I have answered you," said Jesus, "Because of the hardness of the human heart the Supreme Court has allowed this evil. But God has certainly not intended that the union of a man and a woman should lead to death."

Then a woman stepped forward and said to Jesus, "I had an abortion because the doctors said the child would be deformed." Jesus spoke with compassion to her, "Are not all of us deformed by sin in the eyes of God, and yet from him we continue to receive life."

Then a religious zealot stepped forward to test Jesus. "I see that you have answered well," he said. "Do you support a constitutional amendment outlawing abortion?" Jesus saw how the zealot wished to trap him and said, "I will answer your question if you will first answer mine. Do you support a constitutional amendment outlawing weapons of mass destruction?" The zealot was afraid to answer because if he said yes he would be disowned by his denomination which justified their use as a deterrent to evil, but if he said no then all the people would see that he was willing to allow evil for the sake of a greater good just as those who advocated abortion did, so he said, "I cannot answer that question." Jesus said, "Let those who write laws do so with a zeal for the whole law of God."

Later that night, the daughter of a religious leader slipped into the room where Jesus was sleeping and woke him with her tears. Jesus rose and took her outside. There she said to him, "I had an abortion when I became pregnant after I let my boyfriend have sex with me. I was not ready to raise a child and I could not bear my father's anger towards me."

Jesus answered her, "As the Father loved the child in your womb so he also loves you." But the woman cried, "How can the Father love me like the child in my womb when I have killed this child which did no wrong?"

Jesus looked with love upon her and said, "As

much as evil has destroyed your child so evil has
destroyed you. Doubt not that your heavenly Father longs for your healing as much as for the child
you have killed. Because evil has snared you, your
heavenly Father's love is the greater for you, even as
it is for your lost child. God has not condemned
you, go your way and sin no more."

SECOND READING

I consider that the sufferings of this present time are
not worth comparing with the glory about to be
revealed to us. For the creation waits with eager
longing for the revealing of the children of God; for
creation was subjected to futility, not of its own will
but by the will of the one who subjected it, in hope
that the creation itself will be set free from its bondage to decay and will obtain the freedom of the
glory of the children of God. We know that the
whole creation has been groaning in labor pains
until now; and not only the creation, but we ourselves, who have the first fruits of the Spirit, groan
inwardly while we wait for adoption, the redemption of our bodies.

Romans 8:18–23

MEDITATION

(Silence)

LITANY

May the pain of our loss
—Increase the fire of our love

May the pain of our guilt
—Ignite the flame of mercy in us

May the pain of our mistakes
—Light for us the path to wisdom

May the pain of our hatreds
—Awaken us to compassion

May the pain of our limitations
—Enkindle in us understanding

May the pain of our regrets
—Shine forth in forgiveness

PRAYER

When violence poisons love
—May love find healing soft and gentle

When shame overwhelms our hands
—May we turn our hands again to the service of truth

When life brings to us insufferable pain
—May we search for joy that we might bring healing to life

When we have sinned and are tempted to nurse our guilt
—May we have the courage to accept redemption and live as one of the redeemed

And someday may all true loves
—Find eternal consummation

For all loved ones lost to death, no matter how small or despised
—May paradise consummate their lives in joy

CLOSING

Dearest God, since the birth of life you have witnessed every death: not a sparrow falls but you behold, not a child perishes but you are present. When our own eyes wish to turn away from death, death at our own hands or of others, death of our

own offspring or of others, allow us to see your eyes, gentle with love, that never turn away. Let us hope in you. We shall be redeemed and forgiven, love shall reunite what was severed, you shall hold us forever within a gentle gaze. Let us hope in you.
—**Amen.**

BLESSING

Bless the night of sorrow with sleep, and the heart heavy with guilt with redemption. Your hands have created life, O God, that heaven might find cause to sing. Let our sorrow be turned to song and our guilt into a psalm of redemption. Soften our hearts tomorrow, enable us to find new paths to walk upon, teach us that we might serve you. God, tonight, as a mother you hold us close, may we feel your love around us.
—**Amen.**

(Or)

Now may every living thing,
    young or old,
    weak or strong,
    living near or far,

known or unknown,
living or departed or yet unborn,
May every living thing,
be full of bliss.

The Buddha

—Amen.

Canticle of Creation

OPENING

I open my lips to sing,
—**With all creation sing;**

I open my lips to sing,
—**With all the creation of God!**

PSALM

Canticle of the Sun

Antiphon: **Praise and bless God, with great humility give thanks.**

Praised be you, my Lord,
   with all your creatures,
especially Sir Brother Sun,
Who is the day and through whom
   you give us light.

And he is beautiful and radiant
   with great splendor;
and bears a likeness of you, Most High One.

Praised be you, my Lord,
   through Sister Moon and the stars,
in heaven you formed them
   clear and precious and beautiful.

Praised be you, my Lord,
   through Brother Wind,
and through the air, cloudy and serene,
   and every kind of weather
through which you give sustenance
   to your creatures.

Praised be you, my Lord,
   through Sister Water,
which is very useful
   and humble and precious and chaste.

Praised be you, my Lord,
   through Brother Fire,
through whom you light the night
and he is beautiful and playful
   and robust and strong.

Praised be you, my Lord,
    through our Sister Mother Earth,
who sustains and governs us,
and who produces varied fruits
    with colored flowers and herbs.

Antiphon: **Praise and bless God, with great humility give
    thanks.**

Francis of Assisi

READING

For me, my God, all joy and all achievement, the
very purpose of my being and all my love of life, all
depend on this one basic vision of the union between yourself and the Universe. Let others, fulfilling a function more august than mine, proclaim
your splendors as pure Spirit; as for me, dominated
as I am by a vocation which springs from the in-
most fibers of my being, I have no desire, I have no
ability, to proclaim anything except the innumerable prolongations of your incarnate Being in the
world of matter; I can preach only the mystery of
your flesh, you the Soul shining forth through all
that surrounds us.

Pierre Teilhard de Chardin

MEDITATION

In your presence your beauty surrounds me

(Silence)

In your presence your beauty surrounds me

PRAYER

God of beauty,
—**May we love the clarity of air and water which grants us light.**

God of beauty,
—**May we love the fire and chill of hot and cold which grant us energy.**

God of beauty,
—**May we love the life of herb and animal which grants us life.**

God of beauty,
—**May we love the great age of stone and soil which grants us our high evolution.**

God of beauty,
—**May we love the organization of matter which grants us all knowledge and wonder.**

God of beauty,
—**This night belongs to you.**

God of eternal beauty,
—**May we behold you forever!**

CLOSING

Great and wonderful God, may we your children
yearn forever to be like you: to love what you love,
to care for what you create, to become what you
have shown yourself to be. And this night grant us
rest and vision, peace and hope for the morning
soon to wake.
—**Amen.**

GREAT BLESSING

May the clear lake of the morning forever
reflect the Sun
May the great forests forever sing with the wind
May the high mountains forever glow when
dawn awakes

May the storms forever cast the waves upon the
    shore

May the rains never fall but sweetly
May the winds never blow but freshly
May the fires never burn but purely
May the smell of these fill the Earth with joy

Let the desert sing of drought
Let the plain sing of life
Let the mountain sing of cold
Let the Earth sing tomorrow with joy,
    with joy full of laughter

—Amen.

Gentle Our Love and True

● ◐

Arise, my love, my fair one,
  and come away!
For now the winter is past,
  the rain is over and gone.
The flowers appear on the earth;
  the time of singing has come,
and the voice of the turtledove
  is heard in our land.
The fig tree puts forth its figs,
  and the vines are in blossom;
  they give forth fragrance.
—**Arise, my love, my fair one,**
  and come away!

Song of Solomon 2:10–13

PSALM

Song of Night Love

Antiphon: **Gentle our love and true.**

How sweet your lips taste
In the gentle silent night
Have all gone asleep?

I feel warm and cold
With our clothes all fears fall by
And naked we touch

Do now we enter?
The stars invite us to join
Do now we enter?

Longer your love calls
Than all prayers, songs and words
O God! We enter in!

Antiphon: **Gentle our love and true.**

READING

Awake, O north wind,
and come, O south wind!

Blow upon my garden
  that its fragrance may be wafted abroad.
Let my beloved come . . .

Song of Solomon 4:16

MEDITATION

God, in love we behold

(Silence)

God, in love we behold

PRAYER

  May our love be gentle
  May our solitary acts of love give life
  May our touch be welcome

  May our love attempt eternity
  May our intercourse join us to life
  May our passion abide in silence

May our fears vanish in acceptance
May all things join in our love
May our nakedness be warm and free
—**Amen.**

CLOSING

O God, bless our sexuality. In its joy we find you. Join us in its pain. May your life find fulfillment in our loins. May our passion celebrate your love. —**Amen.**

BLESSING

Let the waters bring forth swarms of living creatures
Let birds fly above the Earth across the sky
Let the land bring forth living creatures of every kind
Let man and woman be fruitful and multiply
—**Amen.**

Adaptation of Genesis 1

(Or)

May God the almighty, Mother and Father of us all, give us rest tonight and peace at our death. —**Amen.**

Southern Wind

● ●

OPENING

Awake, O north wind,
—**And come, O south wind!**

Blow upon my garden,
—**That its fragrance may be wafted abroad.**

Song of Solomon 4:16

PSALM

Psalm of the Southern Wind

Antiphon: **The wind blows where it will.**

Tonight in darkness rising,
  tomorrow in daylight growing,
Always living, the breath of the planet
  rises to the pole.

Come southern wind, breath of my mother,
  gentle with the fire of the Sun, my father.
Small I sit within this vale, O God,

the breath of Earth, your beautiful one,
  passing over my head.

Rising from the oceans
  the wind carries the scent of deserts and
    tropics,
  ancient and living kingdoms,
The breath of distant women and
  the blossoms that never know frost,
The aspirations of men far away and
  the salt filled waters.

There is rain in this wind;
  a wide curtain of storm approaches in
    darkness.
I too shall drink of the cloud that waters the
  whole world.

Antiphon: **The wind blows where it will.**

READING

The Way gives birth to them, nourishes them,
  matures them, completes them, rests them,
  rears them, supports them and protects them.

It gives birth to them but doesn't try to own
  them;
It acts on their behalf but doesn't make them
  dependent;
It matures them but doesn't rule them.
This we call Profound Virtue.

Te Tao Ching
Translated by Robert G. Henricks

MEDITATION

Instruction: Listen to the wind, or if it is silent,
listen to its silence.

LITANY

Were we not loved,
—Still Earth has cared for us

Were we not wanted,
—Still Earth has given us a home

Were we not sent for,
—Still Earth has given us birth

No matter what befalls us,
—**Forever we shall remain a part of the Earth.**

GREAT BLESSING

May there be peace in the higher regions; may there be peace in the firmament; may there be peace on Earth. May the waters flow peacefully; may the herbs and plants grow peacefully; may all the divine powers bring unto us peace. The supreme Lord is peace. May we all be in peace, peace, and only peace; and may that peace come unto each of us. Shanti (peace)—Shanti—Shanti!

The Vedas

PRAYER

When we behold our plainness,
—**God, open our eyes to behold our mystery.**

When we are wounded by those near,
—**God, lead us to your love already poured out.**

When any that breathes of life suffers,
—**God, may there be compassion.**

When any that breathes of life dies,
—O God, gather their life into your hands.
—Amen.

CLOSING

Come Holy Spirit, blow afresh this night! Wind of God, renew our spirits. Blow wide upon the Earth and give her life. O God of the Heavens, God of the Earth, in you we rest this night.
—Amen.

BLESSING

> May the Wind breathe healing upon us,
>   prolong our life span,
> and fill our hearts with comfort!
>
> *The Vedas*

> **—Amen.**

(Or)

> Now may every living thing,
>   young or old,
>   weak or strong,

living near or far,
known or unknown,
living or departed or yet unborn,
May every living thing,
be full of bliss.

The Buddha

—Amen

Thunder

OPENING

Open my lips
—**To what I speak**

Open my eyes
—**To what I see**

Open my ears
—**To what I hear**

Open my lips
—**To what I taste**

Open my hands
—**To the planet I touch**

PSALM

Psalm of the Thunder

Antiphon: **Light has blazed forth! Even yet thunder fills the heavens!**

Earth spins in darkness
  beside the Sun's endless day;
A million energies work against the night
  upon this tiny orb—
But who are we to call such things small?

Before we ever invented machines
Darkness and light have dwarfed our great
      intents,
Raising oceans into the mountains,
  calling rivers to run to their source.

The voice of light once spoke
  and the echoes have never ended.
Let us tremble before the thunder,
  God's voice ever ringing,
That and no other do we hear.

For light blazed and blazed
  and blazes yet through the darkness:
Stars from the stars born,
Stars born from the thunder
  that no living soul could ever hear and live.
And yet we here still hear the echo
  and none can stop it passing through our
    being.

Antiphon: **Light has blazed forth! Even yet thunder fills the heavens!**

First Reading

That splendor of light that comes from the Sun and which illumines the whole Universe, the soft light of the Moon, the brightness of fire—know that they all come from me.

I come into the Earth and with life-giving love I support all things on Earth. And I become the scent and taste of the sacred plant Soma, which is the wandering Moon.

I become the fire of life which is in all things that breathe; and in union with the breath that flows in and flows out I burn the four kinds of food.

And I am the heart of all.

Bhagavad Gita
Translated by Juan Mascaro

Second Reading

Allah makes plain his revelations so that you may firmly believe in meeting your Lord.

The Koran

THIRD READING

Jesus' disciples said to him, "When will the kingdom come?"

"It will not come by looking for it. Nor will it do to say, 'Behold, over here?' or 'Behold, over there!' Rather, the kingdom of the Father is spread out on the Earth, but people do not see it."

Gospel of Thomas

MEDITATION

Listen

(Silence)

Listen

PRAYER

All wonderful God,
—**Safeguard the honesty of science in our understanding.**

All wonderful God,

—Grant us time for patience as our ignorance is led to understanding.

All wonderful God,

—Help us accept the terrifying fires that drive us towards understanding.

CLOSING

All wonderful God, you have made this Universe neither timid nor safe. The fires of the stars shall consume us like chaff and the fires of our terrible and great adventure among the living threaten and ennoble our existence. To be chosen by you is both terrible and delight. To live is to die. May we rise to your great challenge; to be so called is great honor.
—Amen.

BLESSING

I shall make all things well which are not well, and you shall see it.

Julian of Norwich

—Amen.

(Or)

Now may every living thing,
   young or old,
   weak or strong,
   living near or far,
   known or unknown,
   living or departed or yet unborn,
May every living thing,
   be full of bliss.

The Buddha

—Amen.

Night Rain

OPENING

Gather in my heart,
—**Quiet before you, my God.**

PSALM

Night Rain

Antiphon: **Companion of my soul, abide.**

Clouds touch the barren land,
    hills melt beneath the gentle rain.
The land swims in this night,
    distant summits hide in darkness.

The song of the hidden crickets fallen silent
    is replaced by the gentle waves of water
    splashing on the fields and roof

Cocooned within this cave of the night rain
   the stars seem imagined,
   my near neighbors so distant.

The echoes of the heart unheeded return
   the quiet strains unnoticed in daylight
   the strands of life untended.

Little matters in this small house
   within this rainy night;
All is well, and all is good, even pain.
All that waits is a short journey to the dawn.

Antiphon: **Companion of my soul, abide.**

READING

What a thing it is to sit absolutely alone, in the forest, at night, cherished by this wonderful, unintelligible, perfectly innocent speech, the most comforting speech in the world, the talk that rain makes by itself all over the ridges, and the talk of the watercourses everywhere in the hollows!

   Nobody started it, nobody is going to stop it. It

will talk as long as it wants, this rain. As long as it talks I am going to listen.

Thomas Merton

MEDITATION

Gently, I hold all things in a loving gaze

(Silence)

Gently, I hold all things in a loving gaze

LITANY

In the darkness
—The day awaits

In the day
—The night awaits

In the drought
—The rain awaits

In the rain
—The clearing sky awaits

In the time of rest
—Arising to action awaits

In the time of action
—The time of rest awaits

In the time of life
—Death awaits

In the time of death
—Life awaits

Blessed be God who gives me all things
—Blessed be God, blessed be God

No greater love than I have been given
—No greater love, no greater love

PRAYER

Only let my heart behold
—The depth of your love for me

Only let me give
—The depth of my love for others

Only let the Earth
—Be full of joy in her sorrow

Only let the heavens
—**Be filled with wonder**

CLOSING

God, blessed and just, let the birth of this Universe,
the birth of your light, fulfill your love. Remember
us, Lord, and all our sorrows and cares; may we be
filled with your peace and healed by rest till the
coming of the dawn.
—**Amen.**

BLESSING

Sweet night abiding
Gentle rain and rest
Blessing
Blessing
Blessing

—**Amen.**

(Or)

Now may every living thing,
young or old,
weak or strong,

living near or far,
known or unknown,
living or departed or yet unborn,
May every living thing,
be full of bliss.

The Buddha

—**Amen.**

Summer Canal

Lord, I think of you on my bed,
—**And meditate on you in the watches of the
night.**

Psalm 63:6

PSALM

Summer Canal

Antiphon: **I will celebrate your life, O God!**

Softly the smooth canal
   flows beneath the dusk;
Sunset mirrors red and blue and purple.
Nighthawks dive and race
   about my head.
I swim, my head swims in this land!

Sweet clover fills the air,
Rushes grow by the bank;
   mosquitoes draw life from me.
Ducks rasp on the far bank;
   frogs soon shall sing
     and stars and moon dance in the waterfall.

Asparagus grows in the ditches,
   alfalfa and wheat in the fields;
Skunks and swallows, snakes and cattails—
     your water gives life.
The night is warm, the land is rich;
Thank you, God, for the river is full!

Antiphon: **I will celebrate your life, O God!**

FIRST READING

Then the eyes of the blind shall be opened,
   and the ears of the deaf unstopped;
   then the lame shall leap like a deer,
   and the tongue of the speechless sing for joy.
For waters shall break forth in the wilderness,

and streams in the desert;
the burning sand shall become a pool,
and thirsty ground springs of water;
the haunt of the jackals shall become a swamp,
the grasses shall become reeds and rushes.

Isaiah 35:5–7

SECOND READING

The reason why rivers and oceans are able to be
    kings of the one hundred valleys is that they
        are good at being below them.
For this reason they are able to be
    the kings of the one hundred valleys.

Te Tao Ching
Translated by Robert G. Henricks

MEDITATION

Be quiet. Let my heart not resist.

(Silence)

Be quiet. Let my heart not resist.

PRAYER

Response: **May we attain such perfection.**

God of Life, you are our humble servant.

God of Life, you give life to all freely and take in death only what you have given.

God of Life, all your works bring forth life; even from death comes life.

God of Life, your water flows through the rich and the poor, the healthy and the sick, the powerful and the oppressed, enemies and friends.

God of Life, you are our humble servant.

CLOSING

Quietly now, night has fallen, and Earth glides on through the darkness. From age to age you have

been our God. This planet is our home, a great mansion given us together. Your waters sustain us, our journey continues. O God, you are our friend.
—Amen.

BLESSING

May the blessings of God sustain our spirits even as the rivers of God sustain our bodies, throughout this night and throughout all days until at the last we find reunion in God.
—Amen.

(Or)

Now may every living thing,
   young or old,
   weak or strong,
   living near or far,
   known or unknown,
   living or departed or yet unborn,

May every living thing,
   be full of bliss.

The Buddha

—**Amen.**

**SACRED SIGN AT END OF BLESSING**

A simple kiss upon the ground.

Mestizo

OPENING

All creatures gather before you, God, this night.
—Let the praise of God rise in the darkness.

May every creature bring glory to your name,
O God.
—Let the praise of God rise in the darkness.

PSALM

Psalm 104:1–4, 10–34, 35

Antiphon: **In every creature, may God rejoice!**

Bless the LORD, O my soul.
O LORD my God, you are very great.
You are wrapped in light as with a garment.
You stretch out the heavens like a tent,
you set the beams of your chambers on the
waters,

you make the clouds your chariot,
   you ride on the wings of the wind,
you make the winds your messengers,
   fire and flame your ministers.

You make springs gush forth in the valleys;
   they flow between the hills,
giving drink to every wild animal;
   the wild asses quench their thirst.
By the streams the birds of the air have their
     habitation;
   they sing among the branches.
From your lofty abode you water the mountains;
   the Earth is satisfied with the fruit of your
     work.

You cause the grass to grow for the cattle,
   and plants for people to use,
to bring forth food from the Earth,
   and wine to gladden the human heart,
oil to make the face shine,
   and bread to strengthen the human heart.
The trees of the LORD are watered abundantly,
   the cedars of Lebanon that he planted.
In them the birds build their nests;
   the stork has its home in the fir trees.

The high mountains are for the wild goats;
   the rocks are a refuge for the coneys.

You have made the Moon to mark the seasons;
   the Sun knows its time for setting.
You make darkness, and it is night,
   when all the animals of the forest come
     creeping out.
The young lions roar for their prey,
   seeking their food from God.
When the Sun rises, they withdraw
   and lie down in their dens.
People go out to their work
   and to their labor until the evening.

O LORD, how manifold are your works!
   In wisdom you have made them all;
   the Earth is full of your creatures.
Yonder is the sea, great and wide,
   creeping things innumerable are there,
   living things both small and great.
There go the ships,
   and Leviathan that you formed to sport in it.

These all look to you
   to give them their food in due season;
when you give to them, they gather it up;

when you open your hand, they are filled
  with good things.
When you hide your face, they are dismayed;
  when you take away their breath, they die
  and return to their dust.
When you send forth your breath, they are
  created;
  and you renew the face of the ground.

May the glory of the LORD endure forever;
  may the LORD rejoice in his works—
who looks on the Earth and it trembles,
  who touches the mountains and they smoke.
I will sing to the LORD as long as I live;
  I will sing praise to my God while I have being.
May my meditation be pleasing to him,
  for I rejoice in the LORD.
Bless the LORD, O my soul.
Praise the LORD!

Antiphon: **In every creature, may God rejoice!**

READING

This man named Jesus had come too close. Why
did he know about her divorces? Why did he know

she was living with a man? She didn't even want God to know that. She looked back in his eyes. They were too strong. She had to turn them away, change the conversation, reduce him back to human size, make him just a Jew again.

And so she said, "Sir, I see that you are what they would call a prophet." Then before he could answer, she hurried on, hoping to lead his eyes far away from herself and to run them up onto something else, like maybe religion, or even better, a religious fight. That would certainly make him just a Jew again.

And so she said, "It is the Samaritan custom to worship God on this mountain. For generations and generations my ancestors"—she felt an unusual thrill of pride calling upon them—"said this is the way to worship God. But you say that this is wrong, that we should worship God in Jerusalem."

She suddenly felt herself to represent all the sacred heritage of her ancestors and could forget for a moment all the scorn they would have heaped on her for the way she had lived. And how good it felt to say "you" and to believe that this man himself was as evil as all she had ever heard or seen of the Jews.

As he opened his lips to speak, she braced herself

for the excitement of a confrontation. Now, she thought, the men of this town will rush to defend me in public as much as they patronize me in private when they see that this man is attacking their faith. But how strangely gentle was his voice as he began to speak.

"Woman, believe me," Jesus said as he seemed to gaze down into her deepest center. "Woman, believe me, the time is coming when you—" The way he said "you"! He wasn't talking to all the Samaritans, he wasn't talking to a prostitute, he wasn't talking to just a woman, he was talking directly to her as if he had seen her childhood, had seen all the laughter and hatred directed at the young girl born of a Samaritan mother and a Jewish father, a girl abandoned by her father because she could only be a Jew if her mother was a Jew, a girl abandoned by her mother's people because her father was Jewish, a girl who hated God for making her to be half of two races, half of two religions.

"Woman, believe me, the time is coming when *you* will worship God neither on this mountain nor in Jerusalem."

She didn't hear the rest of what he was saying so taken was she by being addressed as "you." Had any lover ever called her with such love? She could not remember even her mother speak with such tenderness toward her. And then as he fell silent she remembered him saying something about worshipping God in spirit.

And in that moment she suddenly felt as if she might be able to become a Jew through this man, that she might be able to enter at last into her father's world. Wasn't that the essence of what he said? Could it be that she might be allowed into the Jewish world? After all, this man seemed to be a great Jewish teacher. And suddenly for the first time she found herself wanting to believe in the Jewish Messiah. She could accept such a hope if she were allowed to share in it. If so, she could believe anything.

Flustered and thinking out loud she found herself saying the very thing she hoped no one in her village would ever hear her say, "I know that the Messiah will come, and that he will make everything well again."

That moment seemed to freeze in her mind even as the moment flew by. She knew that she would never forget the shape of the water jug's shadow or the way this man had sat himself in front of her. "I am he," he simply said, "I who am speaking to you am he."

And suddenly she knew what it was to have a vision. She always suspected that visions lay inside people's heads and were therefore made up. Now she knew for certain where they lay, because nothing changed before her eyes, but everything changed inside her head. For one instant in her life she beheld eternity by gazing into the eyes of this one man. She saw for the first time her mother and her father come together with all the Jews and all the Samaritans and all the dark peoples with all the light peoples and all the plants and all the animals. For that one instant, even as others ran up and led Jesus away from her, all distancing themselves from the shame of having been introduced to him by her, all the pain no longer mattered. He had looked at her and said, "you." And in that instant, every misbegotten union, every mixing of oil with water, every child of the righteous born of the damned, every mestizo union of unlike beings had revealed itself to be the messianic moment. In that moment, the very thing that religion and race and species most abhorred, the union in love of unlike beings, revealed itself to be the face of God.

Based on John 4

MEDITATION

**God, it is, who has made all things;
By God, all things are loved.**

(Silence)

**God, it is, who has made all things;
By God, all things are loved.**

PRAYER

Instruction: Listen to and give voice to the prayers of all creatures and all creation.

CLOSING

Response: **Let the kingdom come, let the kingdom come.**

For all the lonely and outcast, those rejected and insulted, those in the middle between warring camps.

For all the wounded and all the well, for all the dark and all the bright, for all the friends and all the enemies.

For all the souls lost, for all the living who die in despair, for all the wounds this world cannot yet heal.

BLESSING

Let the hand of God come gentle down and rest lightly upon us. If we would turn and flee, may peace rise inside ourselves though it has never risen before. Let the hand of God be welcome, let the creature awaken to the love of its creator, let the eternal reign of God begin in the small moments of this night.
—**Amen.**

(Or)

Now may every living thing,
    young or old,
    weak or strong,
    living near or far,
    known or unknown,
    living or departed or yet unborn,
May every living thing,
    be full of bliss.

The Buddha

Homeland

●) (●

Open heart and sing!
—**Here tonight, is not God with us!**

PSALM

Psalm 148:1–4, 7–13, 14

Antiphon: **Praise your name, Creator of the Heavens and
the Earth!**

Praise the LORD!
Praise the LORD from the heavens;
  praise him in the heights!
Praise him, Sun and Moon;
  praise him, all you shining stars!
Praise him, you highest heavens,
  and you water above the heavens!

Praise the LORD from the Earth,
  you sea monsters and all deeps,
fire and hail, snow and frost,
  stormy wind fulfilling his command!

Mountains and all hills,
  fruit trees and all cedars!
Wild animals and all cattle,
  creeping things and flying birds!

Kings of the Earth and all peoples,
  princes and all rulers of the Earth!
Young men and women alike,
  old and young together!

Let them praise the name of the LORD,
  for his name alone is exalted;
  his glory is above the Earth and heaven.
Praise the LORD!

Antiphon: **Praise your name, Creator of the Heavens and the Earth!**

FIRST READING

For I have lit on a great truth: to wit, that all men *dwell,* and life's meaning changes for them with the meaning of the home. And that roads, barley-fields and hillsides look different to a man according as they belong, or do not belong, to a domain. For once we feel that these diverse things are bound together in a whole, then and only then, do they make an imprint on our hearts. Likewise, he who dwells and he who dwells not in the Kingdom of God do not inhabit the same universe.

Antoine de Saint-Exupery

SECOND READING

I love that man whose religion sets free and whose life is quickened by intimations of divinity within him: the kingdom of God, the empire, the domain, his home—so that day in, day out, he barters himself for something vaster than himself.

Antoine de Saint-Exupery

THIRD READING

In my long night walks it was revealed to me that the quality of my empire's civilization rests not on its material benefits but on men's obligations and the zeal they bring to their tasks. It derives not from owning but from giving. Civilized is that craftsman . . . who remakes himself in the thing he works on, and, for his recompense, becomes eternal, no longer dreading death.

Antoine de Saint-Exupery

MEDITATION

**Showing great respect
I call to mind the land of my birth.**

(Silence)

**Showing great respect
I call to mind the land of my birth.**

LITANY

Were it but a tree
—Our hands would pass it by and never touch the wood of the cross.

Were it but a branch
—Our hands would pass it by and never touch the crown of thorns.

Were it but a boll of cotton
—Our hands would pass it by and never touch the hem of his garment.

Were it but a metal
—Our hands would pass it by and never touch the treasures at his feet.

Were it but a star
—Our path would pass it by and never find the god in a manger.

Were it but a planet
—Our lives would pass it by and never enter the kingdom of God.

PRAYER

May my homeland continue to live beyond my life.
—Amen.

May children continue to live in my homeland many generations.
—Amen.

May it be blessed with abundance and health in its air, its water and its soil.
—**Amen.**

May the wild creatures it has born, bear many descendants and may they not be driven from their homes.
—**Amen.**

May the plants it gives life to, no matter how humble, prosper a thousand generations.
—**Amen.**

May every creature there dwelling, especially humans, love my homeland, for she is our mother.
—**Amen.**

And may my every step upon this Earth be a blessing to the land of my birth.
—**Amen.**

CLOSING

Tonight many walk upon this land but do not touch its heart. Awaken them to love that which your love has made and to love that which you have given them in life. We have no place to dwell save the planet from which you gave us birth. Turn our hearts tomorrow to care for your Earth even as you have cared for her, long before our steps were heard upon her.

—**Amen.**

BLESSING

Sweet be the winds blowing
Sweet be the flowing rivers
Sweet be the life giving plants
For all who live in peace

Sweet be the night
Sweet be the dawn
Sweet be the air
Sweet be the heavens toward us

May the forest be sweet
And the light of the Sun be sweet
May the milk of our cows be sweet
And may God be sweet to us
—**Amen.**

Based on Rig Veda I, 90:6–9

(Or)

Now may every living thing,
   young or old,
   weak or strong,
   living near or far,
   known or unknown,
   living or departed or yet unborn,
May every living thing,
   be full of bliss.

The Buddha

—Amen.

Peace Without Borders

● ◐

Behold, O People,
—The Lord your God is One.

Behold, O People,
—The Earth your Life is One.

PSALM

Peace without Borders

Antiphon: **Rain of God, upon the Earth falling.**

Which mother's womb it did not matter
I came to Earth and found her warm;
The seed that swam, swam a nameless river
Deep in darkness, nameless, gentle.

I am born and I am loved;
Great your joy I am given.
May all things know this joy

Of the water and the fire,
The energy of your love upon this Earth,
The light of your glory filling these heavens,
The eternity of all things connected

Antiphon: **Send your Reign upon the Earth!**

READING

You have heard that it was said, "You shall love
your neighbor and hate your enemy." But I say to
you, love your enemies and pray for those who persecute you, so that you may be children of your
Father in heaven; for he makes his Sun rise on the
evil and on the good, and sends rain on the
righteous and on the unrighteous. For if you love
those who love you, what reward do you have? Do
not even the tax collectors do the same? And if you
greet only your brothers and sisters, what more are
you doing than others? Do not even the Gentiles do
the same? Be perfect, therefore, as your heavenly
Father is perfect.

Matthew 5:43–48

MEDITATION

I come and turn, in stillness wait

(Silence)

I come and turn, in stillness wait

GREAT BLESSING

   Bless, O God, my enemies with sunshine;
   Upon their crops come shining.
   May green grass grow in their meadows,
   Sweet crops within their fields;
   Send rain upon their soil,
   Fill their children with joy,
   Bless their grandparents with peace.
   May every woman of them know delight;
   May every man of them be loved.
   May the birds of their air never hear bombs;
   May their rivers run clean,
      their air smell sweet in the morning.

   May all things with life be blessed!
   For if my enemy is not blessed,
   How can I, O Lord, be blessed?

How can I?
For Earth shall cry if they shall weep,
And I shall cry if she is hurt.

PRAYER

Instruction: In silence, hold your enemies, their turmoil and your turmoil in your heart, and allow God to look kindly upon you with love. Look to God to answer. In silence wait.

(Or)

Response: **Answer our prayers.**

God of the just . . .
God of the evil . . .
God of the kind . . .
God of the hard . . .
God of the living . . .
God of the dead . . .
Let God who has loved all things . . .

CLOSING

And now, O Lord, though restless we wait for peace upon the Earth, may peace close this day just

passed, may peace fill all nights of darkness and
may we abide in peace tomorrow.

—**Amen.**

BLESSING

Now may every living thing,
　　young or old,
　　weak or strong,
　　living near or far,
　　known or unknown,
　　living or departed or yet unborn,
May every living thing,
　　be full of bliss.

The Buddha

—**Amen.**

(Or)

Instruction: With hands together and before you
with palms facing outwards, move them in silent
blessing of all creation till they face to your left and
right. Then turn your palms face inward and bring
them back together collecting all of creation and
then kiss your palms together. Bow your head and
close your eyes. When you are ready, go in peace.

Letting Go

OPENING

Dearest God,
—**I come quiet before you.**

PSALM

Psalm of the Wind

Wind, come and listen to my soul;
Come, my soul, listen to the wind.

Delight of the night, come near me,
In your arms the fragrance of all the Earth:
Salt sea and field of clover
Scent of rain and cool of darkness.

Wind that speaks listen to my voice;
Ears that listen, listen to the wind.

Gentle your fingers idle through the leaves
Attentive in the silence of the night

I shall not ever wander alone
With you beside me.

Wind that plays in the leaves of the corn;
Mind that follows play also in the corn.

A dance, and a gentle dance
This life upon the Earth
For all the storm and all the stillness
A gentle breeze shall blow and crickets sing their
    song.

Wind, come and listen to my soul;
Come, my soul, listen to the wind.

FIRST READING

Do not be idolatrous about or bound to any doc-
trine, theory, or ideology, even Buddhist ones. All
systems of thought are guiding means; they are not
absolute truth.

Do not think that the knowledge you presently possess is changeless, absolute truth. Avoid being
narrow-minded and bound to present views. Learn
and practice non-attachment from views in order
to be open to receive others' viewpoints. Truth is
found in life and not merely in conceptual knowl-

edge. Be ready to learn throughout your entire life and to observe reality in yourself and in the world at all times.

Do not force others, including children, by any means whatsoever, to adopt your views, whether by authority, threat, money, propaganda, or even education. However, through compassionate dialogue, help others renounce fanaticism and narrowness.

Thich Nhat Hanh

SECOND READING

Come to me, all you that are weary and are carrying heavy burdens, and I will give you rest. Take my yoke upon you, and learn from me; for I am gentle and humble in heart, and you will find rest for your souls. For my yoke is easy, and my burden is light.

Matthew 11:28–30

MEDITATION

Letting go, my breath grows quiet
Mind and heart find rest

(Silence)

Calm now the breeze
In beauty and peace all things come to me

PETITIONS

Dear God of the Universe, your winds blow on many planets
—And yet we only feel the wind upon our own.

Let not the food we have tasted
—Keep us from tasting other food.

Let not the words we have heard
—Keep us from hearing other words.

Let not the wisdom we have received
—Keep us from accepting other insight.

As we have been bent to the winds that blow in our lands
—Let us not grow stiff to the winds that blow from other quarters.

And for the things that this day has brought
—God, hear our prayer.

CLOSING

O God, you have been the place of our dwelling, through all the generations of life. Before the mountains formed or the Earth and the Universe were born, before and after all time, you are God.

May we behold your unwavering love early in life, so that we may be content and filled with joy all our days. Satisfy our hearts for the days we have seen evil and the pain you have caused us to bear. Reveal your purpose to those who serve you, and your wonder to their children. May your beauty be upon us and all your creatures. May all things prosper in your sight.

—Amen.

Based on Psalm 90

BLESSING

Let night be blessed
and day that follows

Let my heart be quiet
   and my hands that follow
Gently, gently letting go
   to lightly dance, lightly dance
Like wind among the corn.
—**Amen.**

(Or)

May God the almighty, Mother and Father of us
all, give us rest tonight and peace at our death.
—**Amen.**

Miracle

● ◐

The kingdom of God is spread out upon the
Earth.
—Open my eyes that I might see!

PSALM

A poem by Richard B. Feynman

Antiphon: **What can we say to dispel the mystery of
existence?**

There are the rushing waves
mountains of molecules
each stupidly minding its own business
trillions apart
yet forming white surf in unison.

Ages on ages
before any eyes could see
year after year

thunderously pounding the shore as now.
For whom, for what?
On a dead planet
with no life to entertain.

Never at rest
tortured by energy
wasted prodigiously by the Sun
poured into space.
A mite makes the sea roar.

Deep in the sea
all molecules repeat
the patterns of one another
till complex new ones are formed.
They make others like themselves
and a new dance starts.

Growing in size and complexity
living things
masses of atoms
DNA, protein
dancing a pattern ever more intricate.

Out of the cradle
onto dry land
here it is

standing:
atoms with consciousness;
matter with curiosity.

Stands at the sea,
wonders at wondering: I
a universe of atoms
an atom in the Universe.

Antiphon: **What can we say to dispel the mystery of
existence?**

READING

I like to walk alone on country paths, rice plants
and wild grasses on both sides, putting each foot
down on the Earth in mindfulness, knowing that I
walk on the wondrous Earth. In such moments,
existence is a miraculous and mysterious reality.
People usually consider walking on water or in thin
air a miracle. But I think the real miracle is not to
walk either on water or in thin air, but to walk on
Earth. Every day we are engaged in a miracle which

we don't even recognize: a blue sky, white clouds, green leaves, the black, curious eyes of a child—our own two eyes. All is a miracle.

Thich Nhat Hanh

MEDITATION

Breathing in, I calm my body.
Breathing out, I smile.
Dwelling in the present moment,
I know this is a wonderful moment!

(Silence)

Breathing in, I calm my body.
Breathing out, I smile.
Dwelling in the present moment,
I know this is a wonderful moment!

Thich Nhat Hanh

LITANY

Litany of the Senses

Light of the Sun
—My eyes behold

Light of the Moon
—My eyes behold

Light of the Stars
—My eyes behold

Song of the Wind
—My ears behold

Song of the Trees
—My ears behold

Song of the Waves
—My ears behold

Taste of the Earth
—My mouth behold

Taste of the Fruit
—My mouth behold

Taste of the Grain
—My mouth behold

Scent of the Flower
—My nose behold

Scent of the Soil
—**My nose behold**

Scent of the Waters
—**My nose behold**

Touch of the Stone
—**My skin behold**

Touch of the Soft
—**My skin behold**

Touch of the Warm
—**My skin behold**

Light of the Spirit
—**My eyes behold**

Song of the Spirit
—**My ears behold**

Taste of the Spirit
—**My mouth behold**

Scent of the Spirit
—**My nose behold**

Touch of the Spirit
—**My skin behold**

PRAYER

For the city that has no beauty
—May the light of God come and enter

For the living things that cry in suffering
—May the song of God come and enter

For the systems that are cruel and uncaring
—May the taste of God come and enter

For the airs that are polluted and deadly
—May the scent of God come and enter

For the lands and waters that are bruised and broken
—May the touch of God come and enter

For all of these, all I call to mind, and for myself
—May the life of God come and enter

CLOSING

Spirit of God, awake us tomorrow with peace and a gentle smile. May we walk our path with awareness and compassion. May your life bring forth beauty through us. And grant us rest tonight.
—Amen.

BLESSING

Beautiful be tomorrow's path
Beautiful my eyes awareness
Beautiful be tomorrow's skies
Beautiful my heart's compassion
To have life is gift
Let my heart say tomorrow
To have life is gift

—Amen.

(Or)

Now may every living thing,
   young or old,
   weak or strong,
   living near or far,
   known or unknown,
   living or departed or yet unborn,
May every living thing,
   be full of bliss.

The Buddha

—Amen.

Virtue

● ●

Awakening, I behold You.
—**Awaken me that I may behold you, O God!**

PSALM

Psalm of the Living Stars

Antiphon: **O be joyful! Sing of the dance of God!**

The stars in spiral dances speak of joy,
   the turn of immense galaxies speaks of
      wondrous joy;
Silence filling the blackness,
   eternity beyond our sight, forever:
We behold the handiwork of God.

Canyons falling into the rivers,
   the rivers flowing to the oceans,
All is ordered, God, all is set to purpose.
   (Who are we to yet know such purpose!)

From the ground the trees rise,
   their lofty branches rise into the flowing sky;
The tides rush to the shores,
   and the waves follow the winds.
I am a captive, God, and yet I can turn
   in the swell or the storm
   and behold that I am in currents so strong
Their reality speaks of you.

Come! Let me dance in the night before
    moonlight
   and whisper with friends under the stars!
Let me run out into the morning sunlight
   and walk a gentle path,
   the path is gentle in this heaven,
Beneath the swirling stars.

Antiphon: **O be joyful! Sing of the dance of God!**

FIRST READING

Praise of the Virtues

The love of holy Wisdom
   sets you free from all that tests you and leads
    you into danger

The love of holy Simplicity
    sets you free from the clamorous voices that
        surround you
    and from the clamorous voices inside you
The love of holy Poverty
    sets you free from the desire for riches
    the desire for what others possess
    and the worries of your life
The love of holy Humility
    sets you free from thinking overmuch of
        oneself
    and the pressure to make much of yourself
        before others
    and all that binds you to things
The love of holy Love
    sets you free from every temptation to do
        wrong
    and the temptation to abuse your sexuality
The love of holy Obedience
    sets you free from obsession and the body's
        blind desires
    and permits your disciplined body and mind
    to serve the Spirit of God
    to serve your sister and brother
    to serve all people
    and not only humans

but to serve even the animals wild and tame
even when God permits them
to use you for their purpose

Based on Francis of Assisi

SECOND READING

When Jesus saw the crowds, he went up the mountain; and after he sat down, his disciples came to him. Then he began to speak, and taught them, saying:

Blessed are the poor in spirit,
   for theirs is the kingdom of heaven.
Blessed are those who mourn,
   for they will be comforted.
Blessed are the meek,
   for they will inherit the Earth.
Blessed are those who hunger and thirst for
     righteousness,
   for they will be filled.
Blessed are the merciful,
   for they will receive mercy.
Blessed are the pure in heart,
   for they will see God.

Blessed are the peacemakers,
   for they will be called the children of God.
Blessed are those who are persecuted for
     righteousness' sake,
   for theirs is the kingdom of heaven.
Blessed are you when people revile you and
     persecute you and utter all kinds of evil
     against you falsely on my account.
Rejoice and be glad,
   for your reward is great in heaven,
   for in the same way they persecuted the
     prophets who were before you.

Matthew 5:1–11

MEDITATION

Beneath my own pathway,
  behold the kingdom of Heaven

(Silence)

Beneath my own pathway,
  behold the kingdom of Heaven

PRAYER

Instruction: Trust God for your worries and be silent. Give voice instead to the joys of your existence

that you might behold them. If with others, speak
them aloud to others. If with yourself, speak them
to your soul.

CLOSING

God of the night, God of the heavens, all our
wounds and terrors you hold now within your
heavens. Gather our hearts in courage toward rest.
Gather our loves toward you. Renew us while we
sleep, our trust is in you.
—**Amen.**

BLESSING

Come night and bring blessing!
Come daylight fair as well!
Come all things made and bring me blessing,
    for all things have been made to bless,
And of all great blessings,
    may my heart be most blessed with virtue
        within
that virtue may flow without
Bringing blessing back to all things as well.
—**Amen.**

(Or)

May God the almighty, Mother and Father of us all, give us rest tonight and peace at our death.
—**Amen.**

In Memory

OPENING

Heavenly Father,
—**Open my lips to speak**

And my heart to remember
—**The love of Jesus, your son.**

PSALM

John 12:35–36 [adapted]

Antiphon: **Let us dare to walk in the light with the courage of the light.**

The light is among you only a little longer.
Walk while you still have it
so that the darkness may not overtake you.

If you walk in the darkness,
you do not know where you are going.

While you have the light,
believe in the light,
so that you may become children of light.

Antiphon: **Let us dare to walk in the light with the courage of the light.**

READING

Then, taking bread and giving thanks, he broke it and gave it to them, saying: "This is my body to be given for you. Do this as a remembrance of me." He did the same with the cup after eating, saying as he did so: "This cup is the new covenant in my blood, which will be shed for you."

Luke 22:19–20 NAB

MEDITATION

Awaken heart and remember

(Silence)

Awaken heart and remember

LITANY

Come Holy Spirit

Response: **I open my heart to you.**

Welcome darkness of night . . .
Welcome light of the dawn . . .
Welcome stillness of air . . .
Welcome blowing wind . . .
Welcome quiet waters . . .
Welcome storms and rains . . .
Welcome dirt and stone . . .
Welcome life among us . . .

Come Holy Spirit
—And renew the face of the Earth.

PRAYER

Jesus, this night you gave us a command to love as you have loved us.
—**Enlarge our love within us.**

Response: **That we may be your friends.**

May we look with love upon our own weakness . . .

May we look with love upon our friends and family . . .

May we look with love upon our neighbors and strangers . . .

May we look with love upon our enemies and those we are tempted to despise . . .

May we look with love upon the Earth and all of its creatures . . .

May we look with love upon God, the Father and Mother of us all . . .

CLOSING

Humble Jesus, you asked of no one their life but freely gave your own. Your gift, a command to re-

member, transforms us as we do. May your light, O
Christ, abide through this night's rest and brightly
wake us on the morrow.
—**Amen.**

BLESSING

    As the silence of darkness descends,
        let the sentinel of prayer abide with us,
        through sorrow or grief,
        anxiety or pain,
        hunger or thirst,
        defeat or tragedy,
    Till the sure light of your dawn.
    —**Amen.**

(Or)

May God the almighty, Mother and Father of us
all, give us rest tonight and peace at our death.
—**Amen.**

Deliver Us From Evil

OPENING

God of day and God of night,
—**Open now my heart to behold you.**

PSALM

Psalm 91:1–12, 14–16

Antiphon: **Night holds no terrors for me sleeping under God's wing.**

You who live in the shelter of the Most High,
   who abide in the shadow of the Almighty,
will say to the LORD, "My refuge and my fortress;
   my God in whom I trust."

For he will deliver you from the snare of the
     fowler
   and from the deadly pestilence;

He will cover you with his pinions,
   and under his wings you will find refuge;
   his faithfulness is a shield and buckler.

You will not fear the terror of the night,
   or the arrow that flies by day,
or the pestilence that stalks in darkness,
   or the destruction that wastes at noonday.

A thousand may fall at your side,
   ten thousand at your right hand,
   but it will not come near you.
You will only look with your eyes
   and see the punishment of the wicked.

Because you have made the LORD your refuge,
   the Most High your dwelling place,
no evil shall befall you,
   no scourge come near your tent.

For he will command his angels concerning you
   to guard you in all your ways.
On their hands they will bear you up,
   so that you will not dash your foot against a
     stone.

Those who love me, I will deliver;
   I will protect those who know my name.
When they call to me, I will answer them;

I will be with them in trouble,
I will rescue them and honor them.
With long life I will satisfy them,
and show them my salvation.

Antiphon: **Night holds no terrors for me sleeping under God's wing.**

First Reading

God is love, and those who abide in love abide in God, and God abides in them. Love has been perfected among us in this: that we may have boldness on the day of judgment, because as he is, so are we in this world. There is no fear in love, but perfect love casts out fear.

1 John 4:16–18

Second Reading

The light shines in the darkness and the darkness did not overcome it.

John 1:5

MEDITATION

Be still, and know that I am God

(Silence)

Be still, and know that I am God

LITANY

God of the day
God of the night
God of the Earth
God of the heavens
God of my life

—May all things flow toward you

God of the waters
God of the land
God of the living ones
God of the dead
God of my life

—May all things find direction in you

God of the whole
God of the truth
God of the light

God of the darkness
God of my life

—May all things find union in you

God of joy
God of courage
God of hope
God of love
God of all life

—May all things fulfill your love

PRAYER

Though we are not the center of the Universe, we know no other center than ourselves,
—Remember God, that here we meet you.

When our spirits are crushed or trapped or broken and to no other can we turn,
—Remember God, that here we need you.

For all the pain of the living upon this planet and all the unanswered cries of the dying,
—Remember God, we are your creation.

When evil things are done, when we fear the dark,
when we are powerless, when the journey ahead
terrifies,
—Remember God, and stir in us your courage.

When all the Earth travails,
**—Remember God, and help us to walk as your
presence.**

CLOSING

Lord, we pray that you visit
us and our dwelling
to repel every attack of evil,
to bring peace through the messengers
of your presence
and to bless us always.
We ask this in the name of the Christ.
—Amen.

BLESSING

May God be gracious to us and bless us;
may the face of God shine upon us,

may the ways of God be known upon the Earth, and God's saving power among all creatures.

Psalm 67

—**Amen.**

(Or)

May God the almighty, Mother and Father of us all, give us rest tonight and peace at our death.
—**Amen.**

And the adventure of young adults
   in the short nights is forgotten.

In this silence there is none to speak,
   the land lies silent and voiceless.
Silence itself speaks
   in a land grown quiet and still.

Field tools regather rust while the tall grass stalks
   shelter small green leaves at their base,
   hidden as the frost settles.
Life, under a deathlike mask, lies dormant.
In the sterile air, a fresh chill
   speaks of a winter storm's approach.

Antiphon: **Come, Wind of God, upon this autumn land.**

FIRST READING

When the five senses and the mind are still, and
reason itself rests in silence, then begins the path
supreme.

Katha Upanishad

SECOND READING

The bright Way appears to be dark;
The Way that goes forward appears to retreat;
The smooth Way appears to be uneven;
The highest virtue is empty like a valley;
The purest white appears to be soiled;
Vast virtue appears to be insufficient;
Firm virtue appears thin and weak;
The simplest reality appears to change.

The Great Square has no corners;
The Great Vessel takes long to complete;
The Great Tone makes little sound;
The Great Image has no shape.

The Way is Great but has no name.
Only the Way is good at beginning things and
   also good at bringing things to completion.

Te Tao Ching
Translated by Robert G. Henricks

MEDITATION

**In silence recall to mind that which has awakened
you**

(Silence)

Recall the human faces, the words spoken in books

(Silence)

Recall the plants and animals, the humans that spoke to you of beauty

(Silence)

Recall the faces of the land that have stirred in you awe

(Silence)

Recall the talks and silences that have filled you with peace

(Silence)

Recall the moments that spoke without words

(Silence)

Recall the gentle and warm moments of family and friends

(Silence)

Recall the comfort of when you have taken shelter from storms

(Silence)

Recall the moments when death was renewed with new life

(Silence)

Recall and give thanks

(Silence)

Recall and give thanks

(Silence)

Recall and give thanks

(Silence)

LITANY

All shall be well
—The seasons echo in their passing.

All shall be well
—**The birds promise in their migration.**

All shall be well
—**The young promise in their growing.**

All shall be well
—**The old promise in their contentment.**

All shall be well
—**Sunset promises in its splendor.**

All shall be well
—**The Sun promises in the morning.**

All shall be well
—**The storms promise in their moisture.**

All shall be well
—**The Christ promises in his rising.**

All shall be well.

GREAT BLESSING

Let the love of life abound
   and all the living rejoice,
Though the night be dark
   and death be black and full of terror.

Let not hearts quail
    or steps grow weak,
For life has itself attempted more than it knows,
    more than death can ever know.
Let the light of love and gladness
    forever break forth under the heavens
    and through every eternity!

—**Amen!**

PRAYER

As the leaves fall and turn color, awaken our heart
to the beauty of dying things, for you have made us
to love more dearly that which passes.
—**Amen.**

As ice covers the lakes and soon the rivers as well,
warm our habitations, for you have made us to
grow close to each other in intemperate seasons.
—**Amen.**

As the nights grow longer, give us courage to pass
through the darkness, for you have made us to pass
through darkness.
—**Amen.**

As the life of a year passes away, help us to allow it to pass, for you have made us to journey through endless worlds and wonder yet unborn.
—**Amen.**

CLOSING

Keep, O God, our hearts brave before autumn's chill, and let not our hope disdain to trust in the darkest night. We have only awakened in the midst of the journey of life and do not know our beginning, nor our end, but how wonderful is the course we find ourselves upon even if it be but for a moment. Speak in our dreams and guide us in our waking, for the ways of life are wonderful.
—**Amen.**

BLESSING

Let beauty shine before us
   on every path the morning brings
Let beauty shine behind us
   on every path our feet shall pass

Let beauty greet us
   when at last we die
And let beauty heal every sadness
   that lies beneath the stars.

—Amen.

(Or)

Now may every living thing,
   young or old,
   weak or strong,
   living near or far,
   known or unknown,
   living or departed or yet unborn,
May every living thing,
   be full of bliss.

The Buddha

—Amen.

To Abide

● ◑

OPENING

Come, bless the LORD, all you servants of the
LORD, who stand by night in the house of the
LORD!
—**Lift up your hands to the holy place, and bless
the LORD.**

Psalm 134:1–2

PSALM

Nightwatch

Antiphon: **O God, how I love your house!**

O come before the Lord, my soul,
the Lord of Heaven and Earth;
Let me enter into your presence as in a sanctuary,
before your presence let me come.

For I live among children and am a child;
I long to be with you
    as a child longs to be with its mother,.
    as it longs to be with its father.

Under the stars I have beheld your face;
    your light fills the heavens.
I am a child, a child of your Universe,
    a child within your house.

How can I yet know you as a father knows his son
    or as a mother knows her daughter?
I am yet the child, and I watch you move
      mysteriously about;
I watch with awe and delight.

Clouds pass majestically before you,
    the stars pass boldly across your heavens;
Do these know you as I long to know you?
Do these long to be in your presence?

In wonder and trust I shall sleep;
Your eyes my God are upon me.
How I love to be in your presence!

Antiphon: **O God, how I love your house!**

READING

Where can I go from your spirit?
   Or where can I flee from your presence?
If I ascend to heaven, you are there;
   if I make my bed in Sheol, you are there.
If I take the wings of the morning
   and settle at the farthest limits of the sea,
even there your hand shall lead me,
   and your right hand shall hold me fast.

Psalm 139:7–10

MEDITATION

Father, I rest in your presence

(Silence)

Mother, I rest in your presence

PRAYER

As small children
—May we hunger to understand.

Given Earth and this Universe as our home
—May we love you who give us life.

May all mothers and fathers, rich or poor, weak or strong
—Find a way to give of their love.

Forever we need your love
—With patience watch over us when we try to push away.

Guide our actions so that all that we do
—Brings blessing to all generations.

CLOSING

Search me, O God, and know my heart;
    test me and know my thoughts.
See if there is any wicked way in me,
    and lead me in the way everlasting.

Psalm 139:23–24

—Amen.

BLESSING

Within Earth, this small mansion, may the Lord bless us this night, and bring us home to a greater mansion upon our death.
—**Amen.**

(Or)

May God the almighty, Mother and Father of us all, give us rest tonight and peace at our death.
—**Amen.**

Northern Plain

● ◑

Sacred Earth, speak.
—Child of Earth, listen.

PSALM

Psalm of the Northern Plain

Antiphon: **All this land is sacred.**

(Winter)

    Crows dance in a winter sky
        above barren woods;
    Slow winds scrape snow across the prairie
        into silent drifts.
    A cold clear sky, empty and blue,
        quieting into purple and grey,

Lies across the frozen lakes;
   day settles into night.

(Early Spring)

Gentle rains fall like yesterday;
The drifts and gloom of winter slowly melt.
Sadly spring grasses slowly appear
   beneath the dreary sky.
With the passage of the day small patches of
     snow
   will vanish upon the green carpet.

(Spring)

Mosquitoes and black flies swarm randomly in
     the air;
The rasp of ducks among the reeds
   drifts with the breeze.
V's of geese steadily pulling
   across the endless plain
   disappear to the north;
The hush of empty breeze returns.

(Summer)

The shadows of wind pass in waves
    across the tall grasses.
The air is heavy with warmth and moisture,
    thunder dimly calls from the northwest;
A roll cloud will pass in the hour
    and sheets of rain will fall.

(Autumn)

Cool air, sweet and fresh sings in the cattails
    as the warm Sun shines
    through the wide blue sky.
Brown corn stalks cackle stiffly
    awaiting the harvest.
Rabbits quietly browse the still green growth.

(Late Fall)

Cold rains turn to snow,
Grey rivers gather ice.
Sunsets turn brown and orange,
    settling early in the evening;

The last great v's of geese sing of their passing
　　as they vanish like thin clouds into the dusk.
　　Winter returns.

Antiphon: **All this land is sacred.**

First Reading

We did not think of the great open plains, the beautiful rolling hills and winding streams with tangled growth as "wild." Only to the white man was nature "wilderness" and only to him was the land "infested" with "wild" animals and "savage" people. To us it was tame.

Earth was bountiful and we were surrounded with the blessings of the Great Mystery. Not until the hairy man from the east came and with brutal frenzy heaped injustices upon us and the families we loved was it "wild" for us.

When the very animals of the forest began fleeing from his approach then it was the "wild west" began.

Chief Luther Standing Bear

SECOND READING

Every part of this soil is sacred, in the estimation of my people. Every hillside, every valley, every plain and grove, has been hallowed by some sad or happy event in days long vanished. Even the rocks, which seem to be dumb and dead as they swelter in the Sun along the silent shore thrill with memories of stirring events connected with the lives of my people, and the very dust upon which you now stand responds more lovingly to their footsteps than to yours, because it is rich with the dust of our ancestors and our bare feet are conscious of the sympathetic touch.

Chief Seattle

THIRD READING

Now this is what we believe. The Mother of us all is Earth. The Father is the Sun. The Grandfather is the Creator who bathed us with his mind and gave life to all things. The Brother is the beasts and trees. The Sister is that with wings. We are the children of Earth and do it no harm in any way. Nor do we offend the Sun by not greeting it at dawn. We praise our Grandfather for his creation. We share the same breath together—the beasts, the trees, the birds, the human.

Nancy Wood

MEDITATION

Behold

(Silence)

Behold

PRAYER

May we realize our relationship and our oneness
—With the Universe and all its powers.

May we recognize and behold our origin
—In the depths of the Origin of all.

May we find ourselves always
—In the center of your Spirit.

CLOSING

Grant to us the courage to behold the face of the
Universe, to let go of the faces of our comforts, and
to behold the true face of God. In our falling, may
we always meet your rising, and in our dwelling
upon the land, may we always see your face.
—**Amen.**

BLESSING

May our eyes behold the sacred,
   wherever the sacred may dwell.
May our hearts hold sacred
   whatever the sacred inhabits.
May our hands touch the sacred
   and with reverence know its touch.
May our lips fall silent
   until the sacred is honored.
And may our minds attain
   that we might love all that is holy.

—**Amen.**

(Or)

Now may every living thing,
   young or old,
   weak or strong,
   living near or far,
   known or unknown,
   living or departed or yet unborn,
May every living thing,
   be full of bliss.

The Buddha

—Amen.

Sister Death

●　●

Praised be you, my Lord, through our Sister Bodily
Death
—From whom no living thing can escape.

St. Francis of Assisi

PSALM

Psalm 116:1–15

Antiphon: **The faithfulness of God endures forever.**

I love the LORD, because he has heard
  my voice and my supplications.
Because he has inclined his ear to me,
  therefore I will call on him as long as I live.
The snares of death encompassed me;

the pangs of Sheol laid hold on me;
    I suffered distress and anguish.
Then I called on the name of the LORD:
    "O LORD, I pray, save my life!"

Gracious is the LORD, and righteous;
    our God is merciful.
The LORD protects the simple;
    when I was brought low, he saved me.
Return, O my soul, to your rest,
    for the LORD has dealt bountifully with you.

For you have delivered my soul from death,
    my eyes from tears,
    my feet from stumbling.
I walk before the LORD
    in the land of the living.
I kept my faith, even when I said,
    "I am greatly afflicted";
I said in my consternation,
    "Everyone is a liar."

What shall I return to the LORD
    for all his bounty to me?
I will lift up the cup of salvation
    and call on the name of the LORD,
I will pay my vows to the LORD
    in the presence of all his people.

Precious in the sight of the LORD
    is the death of his faithful ones.

Antiphon: **The faithfulness of God endures forever.**

FIRST READING

The true men of old
Knew no lust for life,
No dread of death.
Their entrance was without gladness,
Their exit, yonder,
Without resistance.
Easy come, easy go.
They did not forget where from,
Nor ask where to,
Nor drive grimly forward
Fighting their way through life.
They took life as it came, gladly;
Took death as it came, without care. . . .

The Way of Chuang Tzu
Thomas Merton

SECOND READING

Life is ending? God gives another.
Admit the finite. Praise the infinite.

Love is a spring. Submerge.
Every separate drop, a new life.

Rumi

THIRD READING

So we do not lose heart. Even though our outer
nature is wasting away, our inner nature is being
renewed day by day. For this slight momentary af-
fliction is preparing us for an eternal weight of glory
beyond all measure, because we look not at what
can be seen; for what can be seen is temporary, but
what cannot be seen is eternal.

2 Corinthians 4:16–18

MEDITATION

**Praised be you, my Lord, through our Sister Bodily
Death**

(Silence)

**Praised be you, my Lord, through our Sister Bodily
Death**

Francis of Assisi

LITANY

Response: **I share in life and death.**

With the birds of the air . . .
With the plants of the soil . . .
With the rivers and oceans . . .
With the mountains and continents . . .
With the stars of the heavens . . .

Light has shone in our darkness.
—Great is our hope!

May the love of God shine forth
—In eternity blazing.

PRAYER

Loving Mother,
—We call to mind all we love.

In your hands
**—We place all who have gone, both living and
dead.**

Loving Mother,
—Care for the dying.

And care for our grieving:
—May we be led to life.

Loving Mother,
—Death shall overtake us all;

Remember us,
—And may we find eternal life,

For our deepest joy
—Is that we might forever love the Light.

CLOSING

O Lord, may the end of my life be the best of it; may
my closing acts be my best acts, and may the best of
my days be the day when I shall meet you.
—Amen.

A Muslim Prayer

BLESSING

God will keep you from all evil;
God will keep your life.

God will keep your going out and your coming in
   from this time on and forevermore.
—**Amen.**

(Or)

May God the almighty, Mother and Father of us
all, give us rest tonight and peace at our death.
—**Amen.**

Gentle Our God and True

OPENING

God was pleased to reconcile to himself all things,
whether on Earth or in Heaven.
—**May we be reconciled to all things on Earth and
in Heaven as well.**

PSALM

Psalm of Gathering

Antiphon: **Shepherd of Love, gather together.**

Gather together, O God of the Universes,
   O God of the Eternities, O God of the
      Infinities;
Gather together, O God of all names and Gods,
   God of all shadows and lights,
   God of all mysteries;

Gather together, O God, all things
    to worship you and sing your praise.

Gather together, all light and all darkness
Let them behold the wonder of God and
    worship;
Gather together, all energy and all matter
Let them behold the wonder of God and
    worship.

Gather together the planets and the stars,
    the galaxies and the quasars,
    the nebulas and the supernovas,
    the black holes and all of the mysteries,
Gather together the particles and the
    subparticles,
    the atoms and the molecules,
    the forces and the orders,
Let them behold the wonder of God and
    worship.

Gather together the fossils and the lost,
    the dead and the unknown,
Let them behold the wonder of God and
    worship.

Gather together the futures and the uncreated,
   the promises and the perils,
   the chaos and the creation,
   the explosion and the gravity,
Let them behold the wonder of God and
     worship.

Gather together the stones and the elements,
   the liquids and the vapors,
   the clouds and the skies,
   the currents and the convections,
Let them behold the wonder of God and
     worship.

Gather together the comets and the continents,
   the oceans and the rivers,
   the volcanoes and the sediments,
Let them behold the wonder of God and
     worship.

Gather together the microbes and the bacteria,
Let them behold the wonder of God and
     worship.

Gather together the plants and the animals,
   the insects and the ecosystems,
   the intelligent and the instinctive,

Let them behold the wonder of God and
  worship.

Gather together the spirits of the east and the
  south,
  the spirits of the west and the north,
  the beings of myth and the creatures of visions,
Let them behold the wonder of God and
  worship.

Gather together the angels and the archangels,
  the gods and the goddesses,
  the demons and the dragons,
Let them behold the wonder of God and
  worship.

Gather together, O God, and let all be filled
  with reverence,
  for great is your creation, O God;
  beyond all knowing you have made it terrible
  and filled with awe,
  dread and full of wonder.
May joy be the consummation and bliss the
  communion!

Gather together, O God, gather together!

Antiphon: **Shepherd of Love, gather together.**

FIRST READING

And I heard a loud voice from the throne saying,

> "See, the home of God is among mortals.
> He will dwell with them as their God;
>> they will be his peoples,
>> and God himself will be with them;
>> he will wipe every tear from their eyes.
> Death will be no more;
>> mourning and crying and pain will be no
>>> more,
>> for the first things have passed away."

And the one who was seated on the throne said, "See, I am making all things new." Also he said, "Write this, for these words are trustworthy and true." Then he said to me, "It is done! I am the Alpha and the Omega, the beginning and the end. To the thirsty I will give water as a gift from the spring of the water of life. Those who conquer will inherit these things, and I will be their God and they will be my children."

Revelation 21:3–7

SECOND READING

I consider that the sufferings of this present time are not worth comparing with the glory about to be revealed to us. For the creation waits with eager longing for the revealing of the children of God; for the creation was subjected to futility, not of its own will but by the will of the one who subjected it, in hope that the creation itself will be set free from its bondage to decay and will obtain the freedom of the glory of the children of God. We know that the whole creation has been groaning in labor pains until now; and not only the creation, but we ourselves. . . .

Romans 8:18–23

THIRD READING

The temptations of too large a world, the seductions of too beautiful a world—where are these now?

They do not exist.

Now the Earth can certainly clasp me in her giant arms. She can swell me with her life, or take me back into her dust. She can deck herself out for me with every charm, with every horror, with every mystery. She can intoxicate me with her perfume of tangibility and unity. She can cast me to my knees in expectation of what is maturing in her breast. . . .

But her enchantments can no longer do me harm, since she has become for me, over and above herself, the body of him who is and of him who is coming.

The *divine* milieu.

Pierre Teilhard de Chardin

MEDITATION

**We too are God's offspring
In God we live and move and have our being**

(Silence)

**We too are God's offspring
In God we live and move and have our being**

PETITIONS

Incline our hearts to the poor creatures
—They have less than us.

Incline our hearts to the voiceless creatures
—They cannot speak.

Incline our hearts to the ignorant creatures
—They lack our knowledge.

Incline our hearts to the forgotten creatures
—We too fear silence.

Incline our hearts to the dying creatures
—Not only we seek to escape from death.

Incline our hearts to the enlightened creatures
—Not only we know God.

Let your kingdom come on Earth
Let your kingdom come on Earth
Let your kingdom come on Earth
—Amen.

CLOSING

Almighty God, may our hearts remain restless until
they are transformed, may our ears burn until we

dare to speak, may our vision disturb us until we are driven to act. May we behold your creation, O God! May we know your friendship, O Intimate Spirit!

—**Amen.**

BLESSING

May the glory of God shine upon all the ages, upon all the creations, upon all that is, or was, or ever shall be. And now, as the songs and visions of the night grow still, let us be quiet before you and know your comfort in the darkness.

—**Amen.**

(Or)

May God the almighty, Mother and Father of us all, give us rest tonight and peace at our death.

—**Amen.**

SUGGESTIONS FOR USE

I will suggest how these prayers might be used, but encourage whoever uses them to adapt them to their situations. Basically, the prayers can be done as an individual alone or with groups of people. If alone, all parts of the prayer are read or spoken by the individual. If in groups, a leader or leaders would read most parts, with the group reading the bold face parts. I also suggest that groups be divided in half and alternate the stanzas of the psalms. It is helpful to sign by a raised hand or some other sign the beginning of the antiphons or to have the leader read it the first time and have the group repeat it afterwards. With very large groups, or with groups without copies of this prayerbook, the group can repeat the antiphon at the end of each stanza. Some suggestions for sacred signs are included, but you may wish to create others. In group celebration, the readings should be introduced by naming the reading and its author, if known. All readings and writings in this book not credited to others were written by the author.

Various names for God have been used, including feminine ones, but feel free to change these to suit your needs.

The basic form of the book is a retreat of forty consecutive nights given below. A few suggestions for shorter week-long offices are also included. However, feel free to use this and adapt it to your own needs.

OUTLINE OF THE FORTY NIGHT RETREAT

THE VOID   Page 21
The Earth floats in the void, as does all human understanding. Even the vast accumulation of scientific knowledge has yet to penetrate the darkness surrounding our deepest origins or our final destiny.

THE SILENT SEA   Page 28
As we move out into the void, there we encounter the unknown, the terrifying and the mysterious. In our fright we call out and are often surprised to find a companion in the void, the Creator, who seems to have awaited our coming.

DOUBT   Page 34
Yet sometimes in the terror of the void we are tempted to lose all faith and to doubt every certitude. Even this doubt, though, is a path if we choose to walk it. In the Christian tradition, Friday is a difficult day, because the crucifixion of Jesus happened on this day. All the Fridays of this retreat deal with difficult issues.

ALL SHALL BE WELL   Page 41
God is also a mother, a voice of faith in the darkness of the child's terror. She cannot give the child com-

plete understanding of what it fears, but she can give reassurance.

WEEK TWO

ONE WEEK OFFICES
(All begin on Sunday)

TURNING AWAY FROM EVIL

SIMPLICITY

AWARENESS OF THE UNIVERSE

THE FERTILE EARTH

POOR IN SPIRIT

THE WINTER PASSAGE